MW00528995

FAITH FORWARD
VOLUME 3

"All of creation is groaning like a woman in childbirth, waiting to see the children of God. As my husband and I await the birth of our first grandchild, this image is vivid for me. We can't wait for the brown baby girl to arrive. We pray she will be a revolutionary lover; that her faith – our faith – in the Holy will propel her to be light in the darkness. We'll have this book full of poignant and beautiful and heart-wrenching and inspiring essays on our shelf as we think of all the children being held in poverty, in racism, in violence, in environmental chaos. You and I must teach them Love, Revolutionary Love, as a force for change. This excellent volume of essays will be our primer for these urgent times."
– The Rev. Jacqueline J. Lewis, PhD, Senior Minister, Middle Collegiate Church, New York City

"The genius of *Faith Forward* is that it's more than one thing. It lives profoundly in the 'both and.' It's both an event and a network, both about youth ministry and children's ministry, both for practitioners and academics. Volume 3 continues this legacy. It promises both to touch an academic/intellectual chord and give you direct practical ways of doing ministry. You'll be both encouraged and challenged by every essay."
– Andrew Root, Luther Seminary, Author of *Faith Formation in a Secular Age* and *Exploding Stars, Dead Dinosaurs, and Zombies: Youth Ministry in an Age of Science*

"At this time of change and uncertainty in the church, this book is a gift to be treasured. Filled with words that challenge and encourage, it opens horizons toward a new day in which the youngest among us become our spiritual guides. Don't just read this book – let its words be an invitation to meet the uncertainty before us with courage and conviction."
– Bonnie J. Miller-McLemore, E. Rhodes and Leona B. Carpenter Professor of Religion, Psychology, and Culture, Vanderbilt University

"This latest instalment is a solid addition to the *Faith Forward* series, providing informative and provocative ideas from a diverse range of experienced and innovative leaders. It combines incisive and pointed readings of the times with uninhibited critiques of youth ministry – and ministry in general – while reflecting on what is possible, beginning with young people. It offers poignant insights into the need for justice, inclusivity, caring, hope, and joy. The book promises to rejuvenate, challenge, support, and evoke; on all four counts it succeeds."
– Reginald W. Bibby, Board of Governors Research Chair, Department of Sociology, University of Lethbridge

"If you are looking for 'ten top ideas' with which to resource your children's and youth ministry, this book isn't for you. This is a book for revolutionaries and activists who want to engage in new visions of how we partner with children and teens to live out faith and join with God in the healing of the world. The collective wisdom of these authors offers fuel to help you start the revolution where you are."
– Mary Hawes, National Going for Growth (Children and Youth) Adviser, Church of England

"We live in disturbing times, when the lives of our children are at risk at home, at school, on the playground – anywhere they go. As one of the authors of this volume says, 'The church can no longer be comfortable in the sanctuary.' Read this book now, with others. Move through the sections on lament, wisdom, and hope. Then find the places where you are called to offer healing and love."
– Elizabeth F. Caldwell, Vanderbilt Divinity School, author of *I Wonder* and *Growing in God's Love*

"This is the book I longed for 25 years ago while serving as a children's and youth pastor. Deep reflection from diverse perspectives grounded in theological soil, thoughtful and practical guidance for being in life-giving relationship with children and youth, and encouragement for the journey – this book is fuel for authentic ministry within the new forms of Christianity taking shape in our day."
– Ginger Gaines-Cirelli, Senior Pastor, Foundry United Methodist Church, Washington, DC

EDITED BY
DAVID M. CSINOS

FAITH FORWARD

VOLUME 3

**Launching a Revolution
through Ministry with Children,
Youth, and Families**

WOOD LAKE

For Michael Novelli,
a trusted colleague and a true friend.

Editor: Ellen Turnbull
Proofreader: Patti Bender
Cover Designer: Mark Novelli, Imago
Text Designer: Robert MacDonald

Library and Archives Canada Cataloguing in Publication
Faith forward. Volume 3, Launching a revolution through ministry with children,
youth, and families / edited by David M. Csinos.
A selection of plenary presentations that were made at the Faith Forward
conferences held in Chicago in 2015, 2016, and 2017. Includes bibliographical
references. Issued in print and electronic formats.
ISBN 978-1-77343-027-0 (hardcover).—ISBN 978-1-77343-140-6 (HTML)
1. Church work with children—Congresses. 2. Church work with youth—Congresses.
3. Children—Religious life—Congresses. 4. Youth—Religious life—Congresses.
I. Csinos, David M., 1984-, editor II. Faith Forward (Conference) (2015-2017 : Chicago, Ill.)
III. Title: Launching a revolution through ministry with children, youth, and families.
BV4447.F355 2018 259'.2 C2018-902537-9 C2018-902538-7

Copyright © 2018 David·M. Csinos
All rights reserved. No part of this publication may be reproduced – except in the
case of brief quotations embodied in critical articles and reviews – stored in an
electronic retrieval system, or transmitted in any form or by any means, electronic,
mechanical, photocopying, recording, or otherwise, without prior written
permission of the publisher or copyright holder.

Unless otherwise noted, scripture quotations are from the *New Revised Standard
Version* of the Bible, copyright 1983, Division of Christian Education of the National
Council of Churches of Christ in the United States of America. All rights reserved.
Used by permission.
Lovers in a Dangerous Time, written by Bruce Cockburn, published by Rotten Kiddies
Music LLC. Used by permission.
Strange Fruit, written by Lewis Allan, published by Edward B. Marks Music Company.
Used by permission.

ISBN 978-1-77343-027-0

Published by Wood Lake Publishing Inc.
485 Beaver Lake Road, Kelowna, BC, Canada, V4V 1S5
www.woodlake.com | 250.766.2778

Wood Lake Publishing acknowledges the financial support of the Government of
Canada. Wood Lake Publishing acknowledges the financial support of the Province of
British Columbia through the Book Publishing Tax Credit.

Wood Lake Publishing acknowledges that we operate in the unceded territory of the
Syilx/Okanagan Peoples, and we work to support reconciliation and challenge the
legacies of colonialism. The Syilx/Okanagan territory is a diverse and beautiful
landscape of deserts and lakes, alpine forests and endangered grasslands. We
honour the anncestral stewardhsip of the Sylix/Okanagan People.

Printed in Canada. Printing 10 9 8 7 6 5 4 3 2 1

TABLE OF CONTENTS

PART III HOPE

A Matter of Life and Death

DAVID M. CSINOS

David M. Csinos is founder and president of Faith Forward. He currently serves as Assistant Professor of Practical Theology at Atlantic School of Theology in Halifax, Nova Scotia, Canada. Dave holds a PhD from University of St. Michael's College. He writes widely about faith formation, children's and youth ministry, and culture, and he is a popular speaker across the globe.

A few years ago, as I was in the middle of conducting research about children's theologies and culture, I developed a relationship with an Indigenous congregation in my home country of Canada. During one of our many conversations, Rev. Martha,[1] the minister at this church, told me her goal for the work they do with children: "Our church is a place to go to know that you are loved and to experience the love of God whenever you come here. That's what I'm trying for." Now, when Rev. Martha was speaking about the importance of love, she wasn't referring to the sort of air-fairy, fluffy, domesticated version of love that we see on television and hear in pop music. No, the kind of love that she was speaking about is a radical, no-holds-barred love that involves vulnerability, trust, and unconditional acceptance.

And this love is a matter of life and death.

You see, something is happening within the community in which this minister and her church live. As much as we who are part of the dominant culture don't like to talk about it, Indigenous communities in North America often experience high levels of depression, addiction, hopelessness, and suicide – and this often affects the young people in communities and on reserves disproportionally. Some communities have experienced such high levels of teen mental illness and witnessed so many suicides among their young people that they have gone so far as to declare states of emergency.[2] So how does Rev. Martha summarize her goals for ministry? It's not to teach children the Bible. It's not to get teens to come to Sunday services or youth group. All ministry with children and adolescents at her congregation can be summarized in two words: *suicide prevention.*

Children's and youth ministry at this church is a matter of life and death.

And yet in the midst of the challenges this community faces, many leaders are working to help one another live flourishing lives. Rev. Martha and others in her congregation shower the children and teens in the community with unconditional love. The young people in the congregation work together to build strong relationships and to demonstrate incredible resilience and compassion in the face of adversity. Where struggle exists, love and hope break in again and again.

You and I might not be facing the same sorts of acute crises that this community is dealing with directly. But there's no doubt that ours is a world under siege. With massive crises threatening life all over our planet – economic crises, social crises, ecological crises, the list goes on and on – our faith can't afford to ignore the realities of our diverse and fragile world. Our faith needs to move or inspire us to get our hands not just dirty but downright bruised and bloody as we work against the tremendous forces of hatred, death, and suffering in our world.

The good news is that God is working in our world. God has infused each of us with a divine spark, a sacred thread that connected us with God from our first breath. And God has given us Jesus as an example of a deep and profound love that resists evil and destruction through a radical infusion of compassion, peace, justice, and wholeness. As we seek to walk in the way that Jesus showed us, we join God in pouring out love on our world. This is what it means to be Christian.

Launching a Movement

In 2012, hundreds of leaders in ministry with children and youth gathered together in Washington, DC, for "Children, Youth, and a New Kind of Christianity" – a conference that would eventually lead to a movement to reimagine ministry with young people. Back then, none of us could have imagined the extent to which our world would change. We knew we were in the midst of a massive transition, but we could never had predicted how much more change we'd experience or just how uncertain, divided, and dangerous our world would become – and perhaps already was.

Since that conference in 2012, we who organized the event launched Faith Forward in order to continue the networking, crowd sourcing, and broader movement that started to take shape in Washington. In 2014, we held our second gathering in Nashville, Tennessee, and for the next three years – 2015, 2016, and 2017 – we gathered at St. James Episcopal Church in Chicago. This book is a collection of plenary presentations from these three gatherings in the Windy City.

Faith Forward gatherings bring together creative and innovative leaders in order to share ideas and support one another on our mutual quests to revolutionize the church – and in turn the world – beginning with young people. We talk about ministry with children, youth, and their families; but we also talk about something deeper than it might seem at face value. We're not only interested in how to help children become part of faith communities, or how to support them as they learn about scripture and Christian tradition, or even how to encourage them in their relationships with God. Yes, all these things matter, for sure. But they serve a deeper purpose.

We gather at Faith Forward because we're called to help children and youth live in the way of Jesus, to be those who douse the flames of hatred and suffering in our world by pouring out unconditional, sacrificial love. If we really believe that young people are capable of being people of deep faith, people who have life-changing relationships with God, people who can make a difference in the world, then what we do when we do ministry with them is nothing short of a matter of life and death. You and I have within our grasp the power to nurture generations who can — right here and right now, not just when they're older — work to infuse love into a world in crisis.

At every Faith Forward gathering, I'm amazed by how the Holy Spirit moves within the community that convenes for those few days. At our most recent event, the Spirit's work was evident from the opening session. Both I, in my words of welcome, and Brian McLaren, in his opening presentation, felt moved to reference Canadian singer-songwriter Bruce Cockburn's song "Lovers in a Dangerous Time." As I welcomed people to the gathering and reminded them that our work with young people can radically change the world, I quoted Cockburn's song:

> *When you're lovers in a dangerous time*
> *Sometimes you're made to feel as if your love's a crime*
> *Nothing worth having comes without some kind of fight*
> *Got to kick at the darkness 'til it bleeds daylight*

Got to kick at the darkness 'til it bleeds daylight.

We are forming lovers in a dangerous time, so we can't expect that it will be easy. It's not going to be popular work. And it sure as hell isn't going to pack the kids into our church. The kind of revolution we're launching is going to upset the powers that be – in our congregations, our denominations, our organizations, and our broader world. Remember: *nothing worth having comes without some kind of fight.*

Faith Forward exists to provide a space in which to have rich and meaningful and difficult conversations about how we can do children's and youth ministry in ways that have the power to heal the world, and the chapters in this book are about this mission. They call us to empower children and youth to disrupt the world with God's love, to overturn the tables and shatter the walls and pour out compassion, justice, and love in the world.

If you're reading this book, my hunch is that you, too, feel that this is what God is calling you to do. You likely join all of us who contributed to this book in believing that the God who has touched our lives – yours and mine – also reaches out and calls the youngest among us to become embodiments of God's hope and healing. We know deep in our bones that one light, one divine spark in a young person, has the power to kick at the darkness.

Now, no one expects that this is possible. No one expects that the God who overturned Pharaoh's power, the God who stopped the rushing waters of the Red Sea, the God who made the strong walls of Jericho crumble at the sound of human voices, the God who broke the power of death's grip by raising Jesus is the God who chooses the youngest. No one expects that it is this God who chooses those who we judge to be the most weak, vulnerable, and incapable among us to do this work. But this God is the very same one who chose a young boy to ward off the Philistine army; the same God who hugged children as he told his followers that these youngsters are the real citizens of God's kingdom; the same one who gave Isaiah a vision of a little child leading a kingdom filled with peace and love; the God who, with all power and possibility, chose to be manifested on earth as a human child. Again and again, God chooses young people to be the real bearers of the most difficult, dangerous, and crucial work in our world.

In the dangerous world in which we live, we who seek to pour love into it must equip ourselves with at least three things. First, we need to name the suffering within us and around us through participation in practices of lament. Second, we need to mine our traditions and experiences and draw out the best insights through practices of wisdom. Finally, we must step forward in faith and bring the new paths that we are imagining into being through practices of hope.

This book follows this trajectory. It begins with four chapters that lament the tremendous suffering and seemingly insurmountable struggles facing our world. Brian McLaren, Soong-Chan Rah, Waltrina Middleton, and Daniel White Hodge hold nothing back as they speak truth by calling attention to the manifestations of brokenness and despair that our world is facing at the present moment. The book then turns toward Marcia Bunge, Leslie Neugent, Brian McLaren, and Mark and Lisa Scandrette, who offer chapters that help us take stock of how our Christian tradition both equips and challenges us to reimagine what faithful thought and action look like in our current contexts. Finally, the book moves to hope as Ivy Beckwith, Eboo Patel, Otis Moss III, Almeda Wright, and Amy Butler remind us that no matter how difficult the struggle, how deep the despair, and how great the pain, we have yet to hear the last word. Our world may be groaning, but we are called to hope for a world yet to be, a world that will come about as we follow Jesus' example and shift our gaze to the least of these – the young people who are already calling us to live in new ways.

As you journey through these pages, may you find rest to rejuvenate your spirit, new companions to challenge and support you, and resources to continue evoking a revolution of love.

1. To maintain anonymity, I am using a pseudonym.
2. See, for example, Kate Rutherford, "Attawapiskat Declares State of Emergency Over Spate of Suicide Attempts," *CBC News* (Sudbury, ON), April 9, 2016, http://www.cbc.ca/news/canada/ sudbury/attawapiskat-suicide-first-nations-emergency- 1.3528747, and Tanya Talaga, "Northern Ontario First Nation Declares State of Emergency on Youth Suicides," *Toronto Star*, June 22, 2017, https://www.thestar.com/news/canada/2017/06/ 22/northern-ontario-first-nation-declares-state-of- emergency-on-youth-suicides.html.

PART I

LAMENT

1.

Raising Lovers in a Dangerous Time

BRIAN D. MCLAREN

Brian D. McLaren is an author, speaker, activist, public theologian, and passionate advocate for "a new kind of Christianity." He is an Auburn Senior Fellow, a contributor to We Stand With Love, and a leader in the Convergence Network. His books include *The Great Spiritual Migration* and *We Make the Road by Walking*.

November 8, 2016.

This is the day that the United States elected an American president who manifested incredibly clear authoritarian leanings. The world changed on this day. For many of us, it seemed the world had become a more dangerous place on this day, for ourselves and for our children.

But did the world actually become more dangerous on this day? Or did this election reveal to many of us that the world was *already* more dangerous than we realized?

I've heard a lot of people use the word *apocalyptic* to describe this moment in history. The word *apocalypse* refers to an "unveiling," and on this day we saw that things many of us thought had been pushed into the past, or pushed out to the margins of our history and society were actually quietly fermenting in the centre of it all.

So those of us who gathered together at Faith Forward 2017 came as people who care about children and youth – our own kids, our grandchildren, children and teens we serve in our congregations and organizations – and we came facing the reality that something dangerous is making a resurgence. We could call it White Christian nationalism, White *patriarchal* Christian nationalism, or White *industrial* patriarchal Christian nationalism. And we could keep adding adjective after adjective. But whatever adjective cluster we use to name the rise of what many of us woke up to in November 2016, the fact is that the children we love are coming of age in a world of resurgent racism, xenophobia, homophobia, and transphobia. When combined with an exploitive attitude toward the environment, it all leads to kleptocracy and oligarchy far more than to democracy. Equally distressing, this resurgent regime hasn't been forced upon us or shoved down our throats; it was voted into power by our neighbours.

And so we share this feeling that something is wrong, deeply wrong, and a whole lot of our churches are fiercely dedicated to *not* acknowledging it. The result has been a relatively quiet exodus from the church. I have a number of friends who left church in the months following the 2016 presidential election. These people were hanging on hard, and were heavily invested in the life of their parish or congregation. But they left. They reached a point of no return: "I cannot show up at another Sunday service where everybody pretends that everything is fine." These friends understand why their churches are avoiding reality and walking on eggshells: their clergy are terrified at the thought of offending those four or five major donors who are closer disciples of the Fox News of Roger Ailes and Rupert Murdoch than they are of the Good News of Jesus Christ.

This is the reality we must face. More and more of us are coming to terms with the fact that this thing we inherited called Christianity has a deep unspoken connection with five centuries of colonization by white Christian nationalism, which has been funded by an outrageous and catastrophic plundering of the environment of our one-and-only planet.

And suddenly, hauntingly, nauseatingly, so much of what we call worship makes sense. If you have people who are plundering the environment, oppressing the poor, and building nations and civilizations based on racism and exploitation, no wonder we like to come together every Sunday and ask for forgiveness. No wonder we emphasize how much God loves us. No wonder God is portrayed as a dictator or authoritarian father who will soon destroy the earth. No wonder this kind of theology is perfectly designed to keep the system going as it has been going.

And when they suddenly wake up to this reality, as so many did on November 8, 2016, a lot of people give up, leave religion, and leave faith.

Meanwhile, many of us realize that if we leave White Christian nationalism and join White consumerist nationalism, we're not necessarily better off. We've just traded one system designed to keep people exploited, oppressed, and afraid, for another. My friend Richard Rohr says it well: "The best critique of the bad is the practice of the good." People like us feel that there is this treasure at the heart of Christian faith that waits to be discovered and applied. So we can't walk away.

The haunting lyrics from Bruce Cockburn's "Lovers in a Dangerous Time" come to mind.

> *One minute you're waiting for the sky to fall*
> *The next you're dazzled by the beauty of it all...*
> *Never a breath you can afford to waste...*
> *Nothing worth having comes without some kind of fight*
> *Got to kick at the darkness 'til it bleeds daylight*[1]

Here we are in a dangerous time – and it's not just dangerous in the United States. We're watching it happen around the world – this resurgence of angry, powerful, rich men, who've started to feel that they're losing a little bit of their control on things. And so they and the people who support them are making a major push to regain control and maintain power. Many of us were feeling as though we were at the cusp of a different future, like we were about to break through into a better way of living with the earth, a better way of living with each other, a better way of living with ourselves. Whether this resurgence of fear tactics and power mongering is the last gasp of a dying way or a major reversal of the trend in the opposite direction, it's too soon to tell. But one thing is for sure; this is a dangerous time, and complacency is complicity.

One Minute You're Waiting for the Sky to Fall

It's ironic – our church is filled with all sorts of different denominations. But despite the sheer volume of them, it can seem like they fit into just two categories: "movement fundamentalism" or "institutional lethargy." There's got to be a better option than these, don't you agree?

This is what so many of us have been working toward. We've been trying to imagine what could happen if there was a new kind of Christianity. It would be a generous orthodoxy that would move in parallel with other movements in other faith traditions, to create a multi-faith movement for justice, joy, and peace in our world. And, of course, there are so many good people who are leading the way in this process, and the folks who engage with Faith Forward – and even you reading this book – are among these people. Reimagining ministry with children, youth, and families is especially important and it's one of the reasons why I'm such a great believer in Faith Forward and so grateful for resources like this book. These folks know something that too few people know.

Physicist Max Plank has said, "An important scientific innovation rarely makes its way by gradually winning over and converting its opponents: it rarely happens that Saul becomes Paul. What does happen is its opponents gradually die out, and that the growing generation is familiarized with the ideas from the beginning: another instance of the fact that the future lies with the youth."[2] This summarizes my "theory of change." We look like failures with older generations, but the grace with which we fail is the legitimacy by which our proposals become the most attractive alternatives for the next generation.

William McLoughlin made the same claim in a different context.

The reason an awakening takes a generation or more to work itself out is that it must grow with the young; it must escape the enculturation of old ways. It is not worthwhile to ask who the prophet of this awakening is or to search for new ideological blueprints in the works of the learned. Revitalization is growing up around us in our children, who are both more innocent and more knowing than their parents and their grandparents. It is their world that has yet to be reborn.[3]

Next You're Dazzled by the Beauty of It All

I hope that the foregoing offers a sense of the importance of ministry with young people. So, how can we prepare children for life in a dangerous time? I'd like to offer three proposals.

PARTICIPATING IN A SPIRITUAL (R)EVOLUTION OF LOVE

We have to help children and teens self-identify as participants in never-ending spiritual revolution and evolution of love. We need to give them the sense that if they are part of this movement of the Spirit, this movement of love, then they are part of something that's been happening for generations. We need to tell them that they're part of a movement that began long before we did. Yes, we're working out the challenges of it in our time and place, but people were working this out 500 years ago, 1,000 years ago; even, in ways I'm sure we don't understand, 10,000 years ago. The development of love is really the story of creation, and so it's a movement that has been going on since the beginning of time. The story of the universe is the spread and growth of beauty and joy and delight and love.

A couple of years ago, I wrote a book that tried to give an overview of the Bible.[4] Something that became really clear to me as I wrote that book was this: if you excavate beneath the surface, if you investigate the layers of sediment, so to speak, or if you study the growth rings of the Bible, you start with rules and law.

Rules are important: don't touch the hot stove; don't feed that dirt to your sister. Rules are necessary for safety and survival. But our ethic never stops at rules. It expands beyond rules to the level of wisdom, where we explore why these rules exist in the first place. As we learn the "whys" behind the rules, we learn to live wisely in relation to all kinds of things for which there are no rules. Sometimes our wisdom eventually makes us jettison some of the early rules. This departure doesn't mean that the rules don't matter; it means the rules did their job of leading us to wisdom.

But wisdom isn't the last step, the ultimate ethic. "I could have all knowledge and know all mysteries, but without love I am nothing," Paul said.[5] The progression from rules to wisdom continues on to love. Let's think of it like this: just as Isaac Newton contributed the idea of laws of motion, and just as Einstein contributed an understanding of quantum theory and special relativity, one of Jesus' great contributions was this profound moral idea that love is what we are really aiming for. Love is really what this life and this world is about. So I would say that the early growth ring is about the law, and it involves a curriculum of morality in which people learn some basic rules for right and wrong living. This is a very early childhood education, a kindergarten level of morality. It's tremendously important, but it's only the beginning.

At this early level, every Bible story seems to yield some moral or rule to follow.[6] I remember my heart sank one day when I was a pastor and I learned that the Bible lesson for the week in our children's curriculum was the story about Jesus going to Jerusalem with his family. Jesus became separated from his parents and ended up speaking with the leaders of the temple. The end of the children's lesson was this: "So when you go to the grocery store, be sure to stay with your mommy so you don't get lost." There had to be a clear moral to the story.

Jonathan Haidt and others have helped us realize that there are six basic lines of moral reasoning. And it turns out that political liberals specialize in the first two: justice and compassion. Meanwhile, political conservatives talk about five or even all six: justice and compassion, plus purity, in-group loyalty, liberty, and tradition. This helps explain why conservatives often feel that they are more moral than liberals: they work on six cylinders, and the liberals only seem to work on two.

A lot of us who might identify as more progressive see in-group loyalty, purity, liberty, and tradition as being sometimes highly problematic – even immoral. For example, if in-group loyalty leads me to be hateful to an outside group, it can lead to xenophobia. If my purity rules lead me to call others unclean, they can lead to "ethnic cleansing." If I care about my liberty but not the liberty of others, I can become an oppressor. And if our traditions are outdated or misguided, they inhibit rather than support human flourishing.

As we help children learn basic principles of morality, yes, we should emphasize justice and compassion, but we shouldn't abandon the other four lines of moral reasoning. For example, we can help one another expand our sense of loyalty from our particular in-group to all groups and all people. We can teach that hate and violence and greed are the most impure things of all. We can help create in young people a sense of care for liberty for all of humankind – not just for our kind. We can help them experience deep wisdom and contemplative traditions instead of the shallow traditions of rules, and we can help them differentiate between a vital living tradition and a stagnant dead one.

These are exactly the kinds of shifts that I believe happen throughout the Bible, beginning with the prophets and the wisdom literature, and flowering in the New Testament with Jesus and Mary and Paul. These three open up their inherited tradition so it can expand into a living tradition of change and evolution.

So yes, moral work is important. It is foundational.

But in a dangerous time we need to move from moral grounding to a curriculum of wisdom. In such a curriculum we can say, "Look, you need to learn the rules. But there's something way better than rules, and when you're a little older we'll tell you more about it." As children get older, we can induct them into the curriculum of wisdom. And then we can tell them, "Wisdom is great, but there's something even better – a still more excellent way!"

This more excellent way is, of course, the curriculum of love. It would start by teaching about love for neighbour. It would teach about all the circles of neighbours, from our biological neighbours to our geographical neighbours; from our spiritual neighbours to our economic neighbours; and to all the other public identities that we have. This kind of radical neighbourliness extends even to the outsider, the outcast, the other, and the enemy.

The curriculum of rules is foundational, and the curriculum of wisdom is practical. But the curriculum of love is transformational. If we teach young people to love their neighbour as themselves, it will naturally lead us to help them to love themselves. So few of us had much helpful training about the right kind of self-love when we were young. When we think about all of the ways that people take in billions of dollars every day by making us feel bad about our bodies so they can sell us products that will supposedly make us acceptable and happy, it's no wonder that self-hatred and suicide are rampant.

This is why we have essential work to do in order to help our kids learn how to defiantly love themselves with a love that defies the flood of messages of self-loathing that flow from our consumerist economy. This self-love includes helping them love their sexuality in a healthy way – something that religion has not specialized in, to speak in understatement.

Love of neighbour and love of self inevitably lead to loving the earth and creation, our communal home. And love of creation leads naturally to helping people to love God and to understand that God is actually known and experienced in the experience of loving on all of these earlier levels. These four loves – of neighbour near and far, of oneself, of the earth, and of God – are intertwined in one another.

If we teach this kind of curriculum, moving from rules to wisdom to love, we must prepare our children with this powerful truth: the love that currently "makes the world go round" is not the sort of love we practice in the church. It is, rather, the love of money. Rather than building an economy of hope and care and justice, such love destroys because of the erroneous value it places on things. We need to offer our children another way to love. But be warned: if we teach young people to be suspicious of our totalitarian consumerist economy, if we warn them about the dangers of the love of money, I have no doubt we will have some people upset with us, maybe starting with some parents. But that doesn't mean it's not important to teach this. After all, trading a love of money for a love of neighbour, self, creation, and God is an essential part of the life of discipleship – it's an educational failure not to teach it.

We also have to address with children and youth the danger of fear, because fear works against love. Advertisers spend billions of dollars to make us hate our bodies because of their love of money. Politicians use the enormous political power of fear to consolidate their power, thus inhibiting love; they win votes by burning love, just as dirty energy burns fossil fuels and destroys the environment.

When I think about this culture of fear, it seems to be a direct contrast to the bedtime stories we tell children. These gentle, soothing stories to help them go to sleep at night are important in their own way. But I think we ought to invent a new genre of children's story – something called wakeup stories. These would be stories to help children wake up to the real world in which they live and understand that this is a dangerous time, a time when our economic system's love of money and our political system's manipulation by fear threaten to undermine not only the curriculum of love, but also the curricula of wisdom and rules. The chemical reaction of economic greed and political fear can, very literally, blow the whole thing up, and we do young people a disservice by soothing them into thinking everything is all right. In appropriate ways, we need to offer wakeup stories so that, as they get older, they have the resources, tools, and skills they need to be agents of love in our dangerous time.

LIFELONG ACTIVISM FOR THE COMMON GOOD

This first proposal, a curriculum that leads from rules to wisdom to love, leads to a second proposal in this dangerous time: to help children and adolescents understand themselves as lifelong Christian activists seeking first the common good that we call "the kingdom of God."

Some of us in this great big Christian family of ours baptize infants and others of us baptize older children, teens, and adults. We also practice confirmation for children and youth, which means that regardless of our baptismal traditions, we have rituals for further initiating children into the church when they are older and can choose for themselves. I sometimes think that if we were doing our job with these coming-of-age practices – whether baptism or confirmation – we'd find that many might walk away *before* they go through these rituals saying, "No, sorry. This isn't the life for me."

If we were doing our job, we'd ask them tough questions and engage in tough conversations. Do you want to be a loving person? Do you want to join in the vital spiritual activism of authentic faith? Do you want to join God in the healing of the world? If you don't want to, you don't have to, and now is the time to opt out. Because spiritual activism is what this life is about in this dangerous time. If you are baptized or confirmed or whatever, you'll be involved in lifelong environmental activism. You'll be involved in lifelong solidarity with the poor, the other, the vulnerable. You'll be lifelong agents of peace, lifelong lovers of people with no exceptions.

This would be our curriculum for young people, and it would involve more than simply teaching them *about* this sort of love and spiritual activism as some kind of theory; it would involve actually *equipping* them to practice it, to live it out. What would this curriculum look like if we made a list or a blueprint of what we wanted young people to be able to do by the time they were 12 years old, or how we expected them to be agents of love in the world when they were 17 or 18? By the time they went out into the world as adults, they would be equipped for lifelong spiritual activism in the cause and mission of God. Of course, it wouldn't stop when they become adults; there's still more to learn in our 20s and 30s and 50s and 80s, and many of us know we're never actually done learning how to live in the kingdom of God.

Many people are aware that the word *Christian* has been debased, and some even claim that the term is already unsalvageable. But I want to reclaim the term Christian to denote someone who is a lifelong spiritual activist in the way of Christ, in the way of the saints. (By "saints," I mean we have to go through a sorting process to determine which of the saints are really worth celebrating as we move forward, because some of our so-called saints set pretty bad examples, and it's time for us to move them to the back row while celebrating those whose lives echoed the way of Christ.) Along with saints of the past, we need to ask who the living heroes are, those whom we want to lift up as models.

Obviously, if we *really* want to support this curriculum for children and youth in a dangerous time, we've got to assist parents and families by providing tools for the most challenging work they'll ever do. In my experience, there is nothing I have done in my life that was more significant or challenging than parenthood. Of course, it's relatively easy to become a parent and there's definitely some pleasure involved in it. But the actual work of being a parent for 18 years and more is one of life's most important challenges. And parents need the help of the church.

Since that election day in November 2016, when many of us had our eyes opened to the dangerous time in which we live, several people have approached me to say that we need a progressive Christian "Focus on the Family" – a resource or network that helps parents in practical ways as they seek to raise their children as spiritual activists. We need to provide parents with age-specific guidance through the journey of parenthood, guidance that's psychologically-informed and research-based. A program like this would have to be interactive, inviting people to ask their honest questions and bring their real problems. It would have to integrate a "focus on the family" with a "focus on the community" and a "focus on the environment" and a "focus on the world" because families don't exist in a vacuum. Putting this down on paper gets me excited about the possibilities that people who read this book can imagine into being!

So my first proposal is that we teach kids a curriculum that leads from rules to wisdom to love. And my second proposal is that our end goal is to form lifelong spiritual activists, also known as disciples, also known as authentic Christians.

PRACTICES FOR A LIFETIME OF FAITH

Finally, I propose that in these dangerous times we must teach our young spiritual activists those contemplative and spiritual practices that will sustain them through a lifetime. People often ask me what practices have been most important for me, and this seems to be a natural starting point in my thinking about what we would need to teach children and adolescents today.

At some point, I learned the importance of self-examination: of paying attention to what was happening in my soul, of noticing whether I'm going a little sour or veering into fear, if I'm becoming a little aggressive or somewhat complacent. I learned the practice of self-examination through journalling. We can teach this practice to even young children, who can express their inner lives through pictures if they are not yet able to do so in writing.

Journalling also played a key role in my learning around prayer. I must admit that I hated hearing sermons on prayer. Every sermon I heard about prayer actually made it harder for me to pray. Preachers always quantified prayer, turning it into a pass-fail test: "Are you doing it enough?" or "Are you doing it the right way and following the one right formula?" I'll never forget when a friend of mine gave me one of those little black-and-white notebooks from the drugstore and showed me how each day he would put the date on a page and write a prayer, taking note of whatever he was thinking and feeling. I was 18 years old and I couldn't believe that no one had ever told me about this before. It really helped! These days the practice might *look* a little different – it might be on a keyboard or smartphone or some sort of app – but the outcome remains the same. Whatever today's counterpart to journalling is, I would, based on my experience, offer it as a resource for young people to keep their inner fires burning and their souls healthy.

This isn't the only form of prayer that I was guided into or that has been important in my life. I remember the first time someone told me how important it can be to be alone and quiet with one's thoughts and with God's presence. What a change that was for me! Or there's the spiritual practice of soul-friendship. One can have a few soul-friends and use what the Quakers call "queries" to examine the health and vitality of one' spiritual life. These queries go well beyond asking, "What's new?" or "What's up?" They penetrate much deeper: "How is your soul? How is your heart? How is your inner work going?" Through soul-friendships that use these sorts of queries, you can get down to those deeper issues with people you know you can be honest with and who won't judge you. What would happen if we adults became soul-friends with some of the children and youth in our congregations?

All of these personal practices can overflow into community life. What would happen if by the time a person turns 18, they already know not just how to join a church, but how to create church wherever they go? They would know how to cultivate a life of faith in community – with people who are like-minded and with people they can respectfully disagree with, and even use points of disagreement as opportunities to stretch their faith. This would be an invaluable skill.

When we add these three proposals together – a curriculum of love with the goal of spiritual activism supported by contemplative practices – the sum is the extraordinary work to which creative, faithful people (like you!) are called in these dangerous times.

Never a Breath You Can Afford to Waste

None of us has any clue about how dangerous this world is going to be next week or next year. But we can see the road we're heading down. And if we go past certain road signs as a community, as a nation, or even as a human race, it's simply going to be too late to avoid catastrophic consequences. Just think of climate change alone. Glaciers have already started to melt and sea levels have already started to rise. The road signs warning us of this danger are already in our rearview mirrors, and at some point of foolishness, ignorance, and greed, we'll be well past the point where the consequences of these things can be mitigated. Cities will have to be abandoned. Meanwhile, huge areas will lose their water for crops and famines will hit hard. If you think we have problems with migration now, just think about what will happen – here at home and around the world – when coastal areas are under a metre or more of water due to sea level rise. We're driving down these sorts of treacherous roads, and the children and adolescents in our congregations, communities, and families – the young people we love – are going to inherit a world that's dangerous in ways we don't even want to think about.

And, my God, if all they know how to do is sing "Noah and the Arkey Arkey"...

What a crime it is to waste the time of kids who are being raised in a dangerous time like this! But people like us can equip kids to join God in the healing of the world, whatever happens.

And maybe that's one of the gifts of this dangerous time: we stop depending on all the structures and systems that we thought were working just fine, and we go back to the beginning and imagine a new way forward, from scratch. Maybe this dangerous time can be a wakeup call for us. Maybe we will realize that too often Christianity has become a bedtime story for grownups too, putting us to sleep instead of rousing us and equipping us for action. Maybe now, the Good News of Jesus Christ can become a wakeup call for adults and kids together!

In these dangerous times, we can't afford to simply say, "Wow! That was a good chapter. I learned something." In dangerous times, after every lecture or chapter or sermon or conversation, we have to ask, "What am I going to do with this? What am I going to bring back to the children and youth and families that I'm working with? What can we learn and dream and do together? How can we find ways to share our best practices and our new explorations?"

Whoever gets elected in the future, one thing is certain: the problems that have been revealed are not going away. It's going to take courageous people like you working with young people to infuse love into a dangerous time. God help you. God help us. Thank God we're not alone. Thank God for networks like Faith Forward, which call our attention to the fact that more and more people are waking up and joining the revolution that needs to happen in this dangerous time.

We can do it. Together.

1. Bruce Cockburn, *Lovers in a Dangerous Time* (Rotten Kiddies Music LLC)

2. Max Plank, *Scientific Autobiography and Other Papers*, trans. Frank Gaynor (New York: Philosophical Library, 1949), 97.

3. William G. McLoughlin, *Revivals, Awakenings, and Reform: An Essay on Religious and Social Change in America, 1607–1977* (Chicago: University of Chicago Press, 1978), 216.

4. Brian D. McLaren, *We Make the Road by Walking: A Year-Long Quest for Spiritual Formation, Reorientation, and Activism* (New York: Jericho, 2014), recently re-released as a daily devotional called *Seeking Aliveness: Daily Reflections on a New Way to Experience and Practice the Christian Faith* (New York: FaithWords, 2017).

5. 1 Cor. 13:2, my paraphrase.

6   Ivy Beckwith has called this the "Aesop's-Fableization" of the Bible. See Ivy Beckwith, *Postmodern Children's Ministry* (Grand Rapids: Zondervan, 2004), 126.

2.

Prophetic Lament for an Uncertain Future

SOONG-CHAN RAH

Rev. Dr. Soong-Chan Rah is Milton B. Engebretson Professor of Church Growth and Evangelism at North Park Theological Seminary in Chicago, IL. He holds several degrees and is the author of numerous books, including *The Next Evangelicalism*, *Many Colors*, and *Prophetic Lament*.

I was a pastor for 17 years variously at churches in Cambridge, Massachusetts, in the Washington, DC, area, and in the Chicago area. I loved being a pastor. When I was a pastor, I was much more of an extrovert. My favourite part of Sunday was to stand at the back of the church building and greet all of the newcomers, remembering their names. I met new people all the time. That was part of my personality when I was a pastor in local churches.

But ten years ago, my denomination asked me to serve on the faculty of our denominational seminary in Chicago. And over the last decade, my personality actually shifted to align more with my role as a professor and less with my previous role as a pastor. So there's been a noticeable shift in how I interact with others. I went from being an off-the-chart extrovert to an almost extreme introvert. One of the times this shift is most evident is when I go to conferences. When I was a pastor, I loved going to conferences. I loved meeting new people and saying hi to everybody and anybody. Once I became a professor, I just wanted to find the quietest room and hide out during the conference.

A few years ago, I was asked to lead a workshop at a massive conference of about 5,000 people. At the conference, I was in professor mode. I did my workshop and then found the quietest room I could find. It was in one of those little trailers they had set up at the edge of the parking lot at this massive church complex. But God spoke to me, compelling me to leave the trailer and go to the main building. The truth is, I really had to go to the bathroom and there were no facilities in the trailer. So because of my biological need, I rushed over to the main building where the conference was being held and I went into the bathroom. Now, the conference was at one of those churches where what the pastor says is so important that they pipe it through speakers into the bathroom. You just can't get away from the sermon or the talk that's being given at the time. So there I was in the bathroom, listening briefly to the main session sermon; a sermon that was very disappointing. The speaker kept repeating the following phrase over and over again: "The sky is the limit, so reach for the stars."

I said to myself, "Maybe the Bible will show up at some point here."
No. "The sky is the limit, so reach for the stars."
I wondered, "The name of Jesus might pop up at some point here."
"The sky is the limit, so reach for the stars."
And that was pretty much the entirety of the talk that was given at this Christian leadership conference. The main plenary message was about how the sky is the limit, so we need to reach for the stars.

The overall sense of the conference was additionally discouraging. One of my main observations at this very large Christian conference was how much the narrative of triumphalism shapes American Christianity. Our narrative of triumph results in an inability to deal with failure. So we reassure ourselves, and one another, by saying, "You can do better than this! You can also reach for the stars and be a powerful, wonderful person! You're going to triumph over all adversity!" I have noticed this trend not only at Christian conferences, which can sometimes feel like pep rallies complete with cheers, but also at local churches – particularly in the worship life. Of course, in this chapter I'm speaking out of and about my home context of the United States. But my hunch is that readers in other parts of the world might resonate with what I'm saying, or perhaps see it as a cautionary tale about the dangers of Christian triumphalism and the importance of hanging on to our tradition of lament.

Leaving Out Lament

Denise Hopkins at Wesley Seminary in Washington, DC writes that the Psalms of lament are conspicuously absent in the liturgical life of the churches, even those that are guided in their liturgy to engage the whole canon of scripture.[1] These liturgical churches, when they encounter lament, often just leave them out of their worship experience. They just don't use them in the liturgical life of the local congregation. We leave out the laments in our engagement with scripture.

Another study looked at lament in Baptist and Presbyterian hymnals. If we were to look at the 150 Psalms – which serve as the worship text and the liturgy of the nation of Israel – we'd find that 60% of those psalms are psalms of celebration that talk about all the good things that God has done. And 40% of these 150 psalms are psalms of lament that talk about suffering, pain, and struggle. But it turns out that in typical Baptist and Presbyterian hymnals, only about 15% to 20% of hymns are hymns of lament.[2] And that's only what's in the hymnbook; the number may be far lower if we were to look at what's actually sung on a typical Sunday. What we're seeing, therefore, is the absence of lament in the worship life of the American – and Western – church.

I took the same idea and I applied it to Christian Copyright Licensing International (CCLI), a company that deals with copyright licensing for Christian music. Every time you sing a contemporary worship song and you put the lyrics up on the screen, there's supposed to be a number at the bottom of the screen. That number gives you permission to project contemporary worship songs. CCLI keeps a record of the songs that are sung by churches. Churches that have obtained permission from CCLI are required to let them know what songs they sing in order to properly distribute the royalties to the composers. At the end of each year, CCLI publishes a list of the top 100 contemporary worship songs sung in your typical church in the United States. Of the top 100 songs, I can find only about five that would even remotely qualify as lament songs – and I'm using the word "lament" in the broadest way imaginable. One song started out, "I cry out..." Finally a lament song! But the rest of the song says, "I cry out...for joy!" I still decided to count it because it's pathetic how few lament songs there are.

There's an absence of lament in how we engage the gospel message, in how we engage the scriptures, in how we teach our children and youth, and in how we worship. There's an absence of lament in the passages that we preach and the books of the Bible that we study. This realization led me to write a book, which was published in 2015 under the title *Prophetic Lament*, on the Old Testament book of Lamentations. When the book was published, my wife said, "Five years of work and you're going to sell about six copies, because nobody wants a book on Lamentations." She's right that Lamentations isn't a popular book. The church in the West doesn't want to spend time looking at psalms of lament or a book like Lamentations.

When I planted a church in Cambridge in 1996, the very first sermon series I taught was on the book of Lamentations. When someone speaks about church planting and starting new churches, people often suggest beginning with seeker-sensitive stuff; doing the stuff that's going to make people come into the church – not have people want to leave the church. Well, it turned out that Lamentations was the perfect book for our congregation. We were very much steeped in the American triumphalism narrative and we needed the corrective of lament. Now, over 20 years since I preached that sermon series, I believe more than ever that the book of Lamentations is a necessary corrective for American Christianity.

Rediscovering Lamentations

The first verse of Lamentations reads, "How deserted lies the city once so full of people; how like a widow is she, who was once great among the nations! She who was queen among the provinces has now become a slave" (Lam 1:1, NIV). David and Solomon were great kings who established Israel as a great nation in the ancient Near East at that time. But subsequent kings began to follow false gods, false idols, and eventually drifted away from the worship of the God of Israel. As a result of their disobedience, we read that God brought the judgement promised in the books of Deuteronomy and Jeremiah. Marauders from the north came: first the Assyrians and then the Babylonians. They wiped out the northern kingdom, then the southern kingdom, until the only thing left of the once-great nation of Israel was the capital city of Jerusalem. Eventually Babylon laid siege to that city and Jerusalem also fell. The Babylonians raided the entire city and took anything of worth and value back to Babylon. Then they went further and burned the crops in the fields and salted the earth so that the fields could not even produce crops the following year. The land that had once flowed with milk and honey was now a barren, desert wasteland.

After the conquerors wiped out the nation of Israel, they wanted to make sure that God's people could never rebuild their nation. So they took the most able-bodied from that community – the leaders, prophets, priests, kings, intellectuals, the learned, anybody who could possibly rebuild that society – and they sent them away to exile (which, of course, is where we encounter the story of Daniel and his friends). The community had been completely devastated.

The first passage in Lamentations speaks about how that community now weeps at night: "Tears are on her cheeks; tears are on her cheeks. Among all her lovers there is no one to comfort her. All her friends have betrayed her; they have become her enemies. After affliction and harsh labor, Judah has gone into exile" (Lam 1:2–3, NIV). This is possibly the worst moment in Israel's history. They've lost everything – their home, their leaders, their capacity to rebuild their nation.

In some sense, we could say that this description in Lamentations mirrors the way a lot of people are describing Christianity in the West right now. We've lost everything. We're supposedly on this sharp decline. We're at a place where our status as the upholders of virtue and values has clearly been challenged in American society. We're dealing with the reality of what feels like a fall from grace, a fall from the towering heights, a moment when Christianity, in the United States especially, feels like it's on its last breath.

At the time of the exile, the people of God had several potential responses, two of which I want to highlight. The first was to run away and hide. They were in Babylon, an evil and wicked city, and they could opt to disengage, run away, bury their heads in the sand, and have nothing to do with the world around them. The second option, which I think is what God was calling the people to in Lamentations, was to enter into the moment and to experience a period of lament.

How might these options help us reflect on what God is calling us to in the midst of the major changes we're experiencing in the church and in the world at large?

We read in Jeremiah 29:5–7 that God tells an Israel in exile, "Build houses and settle down; plant gardens and eat what they produce. Marry and have sons and daughters; find wives for your sons and give your daughters in marriage, so that they too may have sons and daughters. Increase in number there; do not decrease. Also, seek the peace and prosperity of the city to which I have carried you into exile. Pray to the Lord for it, because if it prospers, you too will prosper" (NIV). The first thing to note is that on almost every other occasion when God tells the people to seek the peace of a city, God is speaking of Jerusalem. This passage is one of the very few occasions when that formula is turned around, and God actually says not to seek the peace and prosperity of Jerusalem, but of Babylon. Of all places in the world, the exiles are called to seek the peace and prosperity of Babylon. In other words, God tells them they aren't allowed to run away. Even in the midst of what they may believe is the most wicked city in the world, they are not allowed to run away and hide. That is not an option for God's people.

The sad part is that a key theme in American church history has been that when difficult situations arise, the church has usually turned around and fled. When challenges to the church in the United States arise, most of our history indicates that we are so fearful, so caught up in our own needs that our first response is, "Let's get out of here! *Let's abandon the world.* Let's turn around and flee." We in the American church have a long history of doing exactly that. When troubles arise, we've run away. We've hidden. We've done exactly the opposite of what Jeremiah 29:5–7 tells us to do.

From Beacon Street to South Side Chicago to the Suburbs

Let me give you an example. When the ship that carried John Winthrop, who became the first governor of Massachusetts, first dropped anchor in Massachusetts Bay, Winthrop looked across at what would eventually become the great city of Boston. In a sermon called "A Model of Christian Charity," Winthrop declared that he envisioned a city set on a hill. He dreamed that this American continent and the cities of this continent would become places where the light of the gospel would go forth; that they would become the centre of White Anglo-Saxon Protestant life and be beacons of light for the whole world. That's why, if you go to Boston today, one of the major streets you can walk down is called Beacon Street, and one of the key neighbourhoods is called Beacon Hill. These names reflect the assumption of Western colonizers that they would take the light of White Anglo-Saxon Protestantism all over the world. They were determined to be a nation and a city set on a hill. Their cities would be New Jerusalems and New Zions.

We can see this assumption sustained into the 19th century as churches become actively involved in what was going on in the world around them. Historian Timothy Smith notes that every significant movement for social change in the 19th and early 20th centuries started because churches were revived and renewed. Movements such as the Abolitionist movement emerged when a group of people read the Bible and determined that slavery was an injustice. As a result, they began to advocate for the abolition of slavery as their faith was renewed.[3]

Out of spiritual renewal and revival emerges a concern and advocacy for positive change in the world. As they study the scriptures together, as they worship God together, as they examine their lives together, Christians seek ways to exhibit God's justice more and more. In the 19th century, churches advocated for the poor, stood for justice in the face of injustice, called for the abolition of slavery, and worked for the right of women to vote. This is the image of the church in the 19th century.

However, in the transition from the 19th to the 20th century, things began to change as the cities themselves changed. There was an influx of southern and eastern Europeans into urban American centres. Now, cities in the United States are no longer centres for White Anglo-Saxon Protestants; they're now home to Italian Catholics, Polish Jews, Orthodox Greeks, Orthodox Slavs, and many others. In not much time at all, these urban centres – which are supposed to be the cities set on the hill, lights for White Anglo-Saxon Protestantism all over the world – have dramatically changed.

As urban centres begin to be transformed, so too does the trajectory of the churches in these cities begin to be viewed differently. Instead of perceiving their cities as New Jerusalems, the churches begin to refer to them as Babylons. There are some old Presbyterian and Baptist journals written around that time that allude to cities as caves of rum and Romanism. An antagonism begins to develop towards the city, which the church now sees as an evil place.

This perception was accentuated by the Great Migration, the movement of African Americans from the Mississippi Delta in the Deep South toward northern cities such as Chicago, Detroit, Cleveland, Baltimore, Philadelphia, and Washington, DC. After the Civil War and the Emancipation Proclamation, through World War I and even World War II, there was a tremendous influx of African Americans into these urban centres. Their communities brought with them vibrant forms of Christianity.

The conversion of African Americans in the Mississippi Delta after the Civil War was one of the most significant evangelism moments in American history. And during the Great Migration, Black churches were established in huge numbers in the northern cities. The first major megachurches in the United States were not established in the suburbs in the late 20th century; they were African-American churches on the south side of Chicago and in the urban centres of Detroit and Baltimore, and were built several decades earlier.

However, even though the folks who were moving into urban centres were Protestants who quickly formed vibrant Christian communities, a race-based fear developed in these areas because Black people were moving into White neighbourhoods. As a result, the White Anglo-Saxon Protestant churches and their members fled the urban centres in a phenomenon historically and sociologically marked as White Flight. White Anglo-Saxon Protestants said, "It is not safe for our kids to go to the same schools as African Americans. It is not comfortable for us to be neighbours to African Americans. It is not normal for us to be in the same church building as African Americans. So we need to go and find homes that are safer for our communities." With that, White Flight landed the White community in the suburbs, and massive church buildings popped up throughout these new suburban neighbourhoods. Similar to the first option that tempted the biblical exiles, the White Anglo-Saxon Protestant church said, "We are nervous; we are anxious; we are fearful of what is happening in our cities. It's time for us to run away. It's time for us to hide. It's time for us to disengage from the culture that is changing around us."

We have, therefore, developed a way of doing church that might, from a pragmatic point of view, work for some. But that has led to a significant amount of injustice, because we have created hostility and division along racial lines and categories. This type of fear and anxiety, this closing of the ranks and circling of the wagons that happened in the church many decades ago, is happening once again. And it's happening again because the culture is changing again. As the 19th and 20th centuries brought change through immigration and the Great Migration, now we are witnessing another shift because of immigration.

New Changes, Old Fears

The year 1965 saw a dramatic change to immigration laws in the United States. What had until that time been an almost exclusively European migration to this country was opening up to include others. In the 19th century the government enacted laws to limit immigration from certain places in the world in order to protect the dominance of White Euro-American culture. One of these laws was the Chinese Exclusion Act, a decree summed up in its name. Lawmakers weren't even trying to hide their intention when they passed the Chinese Exclusion Act – they were attempting to keep Chinese people out of the country. A number of other acts made it clear that the United States only wanted immigrants from certain parts of the world. What happened in 1965 was not a flinging open of the doors to any and all immigrants, but a change in the distribution of people coming to this country. Despite attempts to limit "undesirable" immigrants, more and more Asian and Latino immigrants were part of the influx of immigrants into the United States, which slowly shifted the demographics of this country as a result.

By 2008, a third of the population of the U.S. was already of non-European descent. By 2011, we passed a major threshold – half of all births in America were of non-European descent. By 2023, just a few years from now, half of the children in America will be of non-European descent. These numbers are incredibly significant, and this trend is only going to accelerate. We're not going back to below that 50% threshold of birth rates. We're not going below that 50% threshold of children. These percentages will get higher and higher, at faster and faster rates. It's estimated that by 2042, the entire U.S. population will have no clear majority. And that 50% threshold of the entire population being of non-European descent is not due to immigration; it's happening because of birth rates. So no matter how big the wall(s) some would like to build between nations, it won't change a thing. In fact, forget the wall! Let's build a dome instead. But even if we could seal off the United States, it wouldn't change our level of diversity, because diversity in this country is tied to the 2011 birth rate and not to immigration patterns. And so the folks who are saying, "We want our nation back! Make America great [White] again!" need to realize that they are pining for an era that doesn't exist anymore. Deal with it. It's over. It's done. America is a diverse nation and we're only picking up more and more speed as we go down this road.

The shifts in immigration we're experiencing may be new, but the fear that is being evoked now is the very same fear that this country felt in the 19th and 20th centuries – the fear of what's different; the fear of the immigrant; the fear of people who are outside of "our" norms. In such a climate, we who are part of the church can't be the distributers and the marketers of fear. We need to be the distributers and the marketers of hope. We need to be the distributers and the marketers of grace. We need to share a gospel that is filled with God's hope and God's grace. We need to stop buying into the messages of fear being flung all around us by talking about how we're afraid of what's going on in the world. We need to stop hiding among ourselves and circling our wagons in fear that our churches are going to close and we're going to lose all that we've worked to build. We need to face the changes happening around us by calling out the gifts of God, by calling forth the work of God.

Because here's the truth about what's happening with immigration. As Stephen Warner describes, the new immigrants represent not the de-Christianization of American society, but the de-Europeanization of American Christianity.[4] As much as we might hear people claiming that the United States is no longer a Christian nation – even though I don't think it ever was – what's actually happening is something different altogether. The *forms* of Christianity in this country are being de-Europeanized. Christianity is no longer represented as a White person's religion, because it, along with our nation, is becoming extraordinarily diverse. I'd even go so far as to argue that diversity is happening at a more rapid rate in the church than in our society at large. But while we're seeing greater diversity in the church than we might be seeing in the world around us, at the same time we're seeing extreme segregation in the church; segregation that would not be tolerated anywhere else.

A study conducted by Michael Emerson notes that the level of seg-regation in the average congregation in the United States is six times worse than in the local schools. Whenever I raise this issue, I hear peo-ple say that they don't have diversity in their church because they don't have diversity in their neighbourhood. But that's just not true. Local schools are six times more diverse than local churches, so if there's diversity in our schools, then there's diversity in our neighbourhoods. The difference is that the increasing numbers of our non-White neighbours aren't coming to our White churches. Similarly, if we consider the ten most segregated cities in the United States, we would get an index of segregation of 0.61 (the higher the number, the more extreme the segregation). But the typical American church has a segregation index of 0.91, meaning it is 30 points more segregated than the ten *most segregated* cities in the United States. Emerson points out that this hyper-segregation in churches has only occurred one other time in U.S. history – in the Deep South under Jim Crow laws.[5]

With all this in mind, the questions we should be considering are not about whether there are changes occurring in the world around us, or if the demographics of our contexts are changing. It's obvious that diversity in our communities is increasing every day. And in other ways, the demographics of congregations are changing too. I speak a lot at Christian colleges, and when I do, I notice that ten years ago colleges would have a few thousand students, the vast majority of whom were White. Now these student bodies are still mostly White, but they've dramatically shrunk in size. There's a correlation here: the White Anglo-Saxon Protestant church is shrinking at the same time that the U.S. population is becoming more diverse, so much so that in just a few years from now, if half of the incoming class of a Christian college isn't of non-European descent, the school is going to struggle to survive.

The same thing is true for congregations and denominations. If churches and denominations don't reflect the growing diversity in our world, if youth groups and children's ministries don't reflect this demographic diversity, then many of our churches are going to die. Many of our youth ministries and children's programs and denominations and Christian colleges and seminaries are going to falter and fall because they failed to reflect the new demographic realities of our greater context.

Hope in Lament

This might seem depressing to a lot of people in the church. But maybe there's good news in all of what I've written so far. The good news is that God calls us to a place of lament that actually might provide the hope we so desperately need.

One of the things that amazes me about the book of Lamentations is that significant portions of it – chapters one, two, and four – are presented as a funeral dirge. This is dramatically different in form and intent from the typical lament in the book of Psalms. We might think of the typical lament in Psalms in this way: You have a friend who's sick in the hospital. You go to the hospital, and while you're there you hold their hand, sing a few hymns, pray for them – all with the possibility that that person will recover and leave the hospital.

But when you attend a funeral, you don't use the same language you'd use while holding your friend's hand in the hospital. When you go to a funeral, it's inappropriate to say, "Well, this person is going to rise up from the casket any second now, so let's keep hoping and praying for healing. Come on, in the name of Jesus rise up!" At a funeral, there's a dead body you have to deal with, and in a hospital visit, you have a live body you have to deal with. And you don't deal with dead bodies in the same way that you deal with live bodies.

My argument is that the church in the United States doesn't know how to deal with dead bodies. Dead bodies require the appropriate response of a funeral dirge lament. We, the church in the West, must engage in a funeral dirge over the reality of death in our history. Our history, as a church and as a nation, is littered with dead bodies – particularly the bodies of Black lives. In order to deal with our present situation, we have to address this history. If we're going to talk about growing in our present diversity, we can't assume we're going to be able to fix it like some technical problem. We can't assume that we can simply learn new, innovative ways to preach the gospel, or learn new, innovative ways to reach youth. We've got to deal with the dead body in the room. We've got to be honest about the pain that is in many of our communities.

And we need to be honest about those dead bodies: the dead bodies that were thrown overboard from slave ships; the dead bodies from those who were killed on plantations; the dead bodies of women who were systematically raped and abused on plantations; the dead bodies of Native Americans who were slaughtered in the quest for manifest destiny; the dead bodies of Black men who've been gunned down over and over and over again in the last few years. We've got to deal with that history; we've got to deal with the dead bodies. Because this is part of our story and we can no longer bury our heads in the sand and ignore this history as if it will simply go away. We must be realistic about the need for a funeral dirge in order to deal with the past and the present reality. We cannot run away and hide when we are confronted with the truth of these dead bodies. So before we look for those quick and easy answers and wonder why we don't have diversity in the church, maybe we need to deal with the dead bodies that are in the room. Without dealing with the dead bodies, we don't get to the problem at all. We are ignoring reality.

In contrast to the opening passage of the book of Lamentations, the final chapter closes from a different perspective. Throughout the book, we hear the prophet-narrator's voice speaking out, trying to get all of the voices, especially the voices of women, involved in the book. Lamentations might be the most feminine book of the Bible, because the dominant voices in it are the voices of women who are crying out. The voices of women make up the central voice in the book and, as chapter five comes to a close, the prophet-narrator's voice is almost completely gone. He or she has disappeared from the scene. It is the entire community of those who have been left behind that speaks out the prayer in chapter five. In other words, in Lamentations 5, the people speak for themselves. They don't need an outside advocate. They don't need a prophet, a learned person. They don't need some leader who's going to figure everything out for them. It is they, the people themselves, who speak up and cry out directly to God.

If there's something that can be said about the increasing diversity in our society in the United States, if there's something that can be said about empowering children and ministering with youth, it is to let the people speak for themselves. Let's teach the people, lead the people, guide the people – no matter what age they might be – so that they can advocate for themselves.

The worst thing that the White Anglo-Saxon Protestant church from the suburbs can do is to come in and try to fix the problems of the inner-city church, to tell them how to have an effective hospital visit when they are surrounded by dead bodies. But what would happen if they created opportunities for young men and women, young voices of colour, young voices that have not been heard for a number of different reasons, to speak out and be heard? Let the people speak for themselves. And we, as the influencers of children, youth, college students, and families, have that opportunity to raise up those voices for the next generation.

This chapter is an adaptation of ideas that originally appeared in Soong-Chan Rah, *Prophetic Lament: A Call for Justice in Troubled Times* (Downers Grove, IL: InterVarsity, 2015).

1. Denise Dombkowski Hopkins, *Journey through the Psalms* (St. Louis: Chalice, 2002), 5–6. See also Lester Meyer, "A Lack of Laments in the Church's Use of the Psalter," *Lutheran Quarterly* (Spring 1993): 67–78. Cited in Soong-Chan Rah, *Prophetic Lament*, 22.
2. Glenn Pemberton, *Hurting with God: Learning to Lament with the Psalms* (Abilene, TX: Abilene Christian University Press, 2012), Kindle loc. 441–45. Cited in Soong-Chan Rah, *Prophetic Lament*, 22.
3. Timothy L. Smith, *Revivalism and Social Reform: American Protestantism on the Eve of the Civil War* (Eugene, OR: Wipf and Stock, 2004).
4. R. Stephen Warner, "Coming to America: Immigrants and the Faith They Bring," *The Christian Century* 121 (February 10, 2004): 20.
5. The statistics in this paragraph are taken from Michael O. Emerson with Rodney M. Woo, *People of the Dream: Multiracial Congregations in the United States* (Princeton, NJ: Princeton University Press, 2006), 34–46.

3.

An Ode to Summertime

WALTRINA N. MIDDLETON

Waltrina N. Middleton is a preacher, poet, social critic, and community organizer committed to actualizing the vision of a Beloved community. She serves as the Associate Dean of the Andrew Rankin Memorial Chapel, and is actively engaged in social justice issues domestically and throughout the diaspora. She is founder and organizer of Cleveland Action.

Summertime, and the livin' is easy
Fish are jumpin' and the cotton is high
Oh, your daddy's rich and your ma is good-lookin'
So hush, little baby, don't you cry
One of these mornings you're gonna rise up singing
And you'll spread your wings and you'll take to the sky
But till that morning, there ain't nothin' can harm you
With daddy and mammy standin' by
One of these mornings you're gonna rise up singing
And you'll spread your wings and you'll take to the sky
But till... [1]

This was supposed to be a lullaby, an ode to summer and an ode to the future and the hope that lives in the spirit of our children. Didn't the scriptures say, "For surely I know the plans I have for you...to give you a future with hope" (Jer 29:11)?

Yes. Summertime is not the season for dreams deferred. Summertime is not the season for dreams to dry up and explode. Summertime is an ode to freedom and to dreams and to the audacity of its dreamers.

Summertime – it is the time for dreams to surface and like the tides, rise... rise... rise...!

Summertime is supposed to be simple and just, filled with the laughter and playful abandonment of the future right now, filled with children boldly embracing their youth and all that is good.

Didn't the scriptures tell us what is good, which is to do what the Lord requires? The Lord requires us to, "Act justly and to love mercy and to walk humbly with your God" (Mic 6:8, NIV). What a beautiful act of justice for children to have the freedom to play, to run, to jump, to dance, to swing, to laugh out loud, to stare into the clouds and see pirate ships, dinosaurs, or a rocket on its way to the moon.

What a beautiful image of mercy for children to believe they are human and that their lives matter. What a beautiful way to walk humbly with God, by not forbidding the children to come, to live, to be, to feel the embrace and warmth of the summer's sun...

The fish are jumpin' and the cotton is high...

Summertime is a time for laughing incessantly and running barefoot and jumping feet-first into rivers and creeks. It is the time for dreams to surface and like the tides, rise... rise... rise...!

Now, I grew up in the countryside by the sea and so I know all about high tides. I know how the mud gets thick and slick, and how it stinks and sinks, and it will,

Steal away. Steal away. Steal away to Jesus...
Steal away, steal away home.
I hain't got long to stay here[2]

If you ain't careful, the tides will rise and steal you away from these shores, steal you away from everything that looks familiar, that smells familiar, that be familiar. They gonna come and steal you away from here; from the cradle, from the classroom, from the church, from your community. And the next time kin folks set eyes on you, it's gonna be through thick Plexiglas and steel bars, or in your grave.

Mind the high tides that rise and steal away Black and Brown bodies from these shores.

> *One of these mornings you're gonna rise up singing*
> *And you'll spread your wings and you'll take to the sky*
> *But till that morning, there ain't nothin' can harm you...*

Lies!

Summertime is hot, and muggy, and an inconvenient lie for those unable to be children – unable to be human for even one season of the year.

Summertime has been winter – the bitter, cold-hearted, deathly winter where bodies are left uncovered and exposed to the sun for four and a half hours; uncovered and without human dignity. It places an 18-year-old child, killed by the hands of police, on trial for his own murder.

This is the lament of summer. It is not a hope-filled lullaby. It is the painful lament of a eulogistic hymn.

Summertime is not for the impoverished to go outside to play. It is not the playground for the disinherited. It is not the backyard or beaches or cafés for the outcast.

Summertime is a place for memorials and protests and unrest.

Michael Brown! Eighteen-year-old Michael Brown was left on that St. Louis street, rotting in its summer heat, uncovered and exposed like an animal. And it was summertime.

> *Southern trees bear strange fruit...*
> *Blood on the leaves and*
> *Blood at its roots...*[3]

In the summer.

I wonder if Jordan Edwards was looking forward to summertime?

Jordan was an unarmed, 15-year-old Black youth who was robbed of his childhood and murdered at the hands of the state without a justifiable cause. That alone is reason enough for outrage. Yet the overwhelming sentiment heard since news emerged of Jordan's murder by a police officer was that "he was not a thug." In fact, a parent whose child played football with Jordan in their Dallas suburb said explicitly to reporters, "He was not a thug. This shouldn't happen to him. Great kid. Awesome parents."

Summertime is not for thugs.

Summertime is reserved for great kids, awesome parents, preferably a two-parent heterosexual household. Jordan Edwards didn't deserve to die because he wasn't a thug?

News report after news report and social media posts lamenting yet another young Black life stolen focused on his grades and the fact that Jordan came from a "two-parent home." The very notion that we should be outraged simply because he somehow evaded the labels often affixed to Black youth is absolutely appalling, especially if we proclaim that all Black lives matter. The loss of any person due to racialized and profiled violence calls for our collective lament. Period.

This is not how we should refute the violence against our children, Black and Brown bodies, and human lives. We can't be selective when we say Black lives matter. This is buying into the false projection of worthlessness and justifying murder because society says stereotypes such as sagging pants, weed smoking, poor academic performance, or a juvenile detention record mean they had it coming. Time and time again we place dead Black bodies on trial for their own murders. Enough is enough!

Where can we escape the targeted terror against Black and Brown bodies? Certainly not in the summertime.

The incessant loss of innocent, unarmed, precious children like Jordan Edwards places our nation in a state of terror – not foreign, but domestic. Domestic terrorism is right here targeting pool parties, birthday parties, churches, playgrounds, sidewalks, store aisles, class-rooms, parked cars, and every other avenue of life in order to deny Black people any sense of normalcy.

This is America's summer vacation.

Terrorism is designed to invoke fear and dehumanize the spirit of those targeted. It is unapologetic and brutal. When we perpetuate the notion of unworthiness by first accepting the labels and stereotypes associated with a "thug life," we empower the egregious evidence of White Supremacy and the racist norms of our society.

We should celebrate the life Jordan lived, albeit one taken too soon. The idea that he was an honours student or had parents that loved and cherished his life is not an anomaly for Black families and communities. Why is it a headline? How does the fact that Jordan was among a global network of young, gifted, and Black children become the headline over the fact that he was murdered in the first place?

Is Jordan Edwards' life more worthy of our outcry than Michael Brown's? Aren't they both ours? Why are we stalking the social media pages and the school and other records of the deceased while another officer receives administrative leave (in many cases with salary) without having to assume any accountability for the life he stripped from the arms of the community that cherished his life?

As much as Jordan's brilliance and gifts should be celebrated, we must denounce the apparent state-endorsed violence against Black lives, and place the centre of our attention on uprooting it.

It is time we place the institutions that perpetuate and cover up these murders on trial. It is time to thoroughly investigate and expose their indiscretions rather than forcing marginalized communities to measure "divinity versus deviance" to determine the volume of its outcry. Stop placing Black bodies on trial.

Each of these babies, young lives, spirits, and human beings are ours. They are our children. They aren't demons, thugs, outcasts, or deserving of these cowardly acts. They are ours. There should be unrest, resistance, and righteous anger for the student who got kicked out of school as well as for Jordan, an honours student.

The outrage and denouncement must be consistent and persistent for all until we have decapitated the vicious cycles of evil systematically targeting Black bodies and lives.

Summertime should not be the time for our churches to go on vacation and close their doors. And when we have vacation Bible schools or mission trips or specialized programming, how can we make them sanctuaries for the disinherited? How can they become a megaphone for exposing the injustices on these streets, in these classrooms, in these courtrooms, in these denominations, in these workplaces, and in these spaces that tell our children to wait on justice? Wait until the summer comes and perhaps we will catch a glimpse of the sun?

Too often children come to churches where the doors are already closed. They leave, exhausted by church folks looking the other way as they step over dead bodies while walking into pimped-out sanctuaries with big old customized carpets that read, "Extravagant welcome!" They are tired of the denominational catch phrases that declare, "No matter where you are on life's journey, you are welcome here!" But it didn't include them.

Summer after summer, our children – unchurched, uncalled, unanointed (to quote Toni Morrison's Baby Suggs[4]), and the least likely to be considered holy or priestly – come with their big determined hearts expecting to be the change they hope to see.

They come because they wish to be repairers of the breach. They come because they see in themselves what they want to see in the church. Summer after summer, our children come decrying the injustices that marginalize them and rob them of their future and hope. They are told to simply wait.

What will it take for us to live into our prophetic calling as members of the body of Christ and to share in the work of repairing the breach?

How long will our institutions of faith continue to pat themselves on the back and live off the legacy of being drum majors for justice, even as they have stopped building upon the legacy and dream in many instances?

How do we work to be conscious, accountable, and self-examining while still being complacent and complicit in the institutional racism that still exists in our society and our world, in our communities, in our churches, and within our denominations? How do we practice what we preach and go beyond the theories and dramatic sermonic metaphors we use during Sunday's children moment? Why are our expectations for children to walk humbly and do justice greater than the urgency and agency we behold as their nurturers and role models?

When we as prophetic and faith-based institutions protest workplace discrimination at Walmart and Hobby Lobby, we should be steadfast in also exercising worker justice with our laypeople and clergy and staff. Our agency should be unapologetically modelled in the ways we serve as faith leaders, mentors, teachers, ministers, and agents of love for and with our children and youth.

How do we treat our colleagues? How do we treat our constituents? How do we treat our neighbours? Our children are watching us, too.

When was the last time we did a pulse check to find out the sentiments and energy of people of colour working alongside us in this ministry and calling?

When was the last time we did a pulse check to find out the sentiments and energy of youth of colour, or youth in the minority in youth groups, so that we know that their cultural locations and experiences – good and bad – are heard, affirmed, and are not being made invisible for our comfort or our convenience?

How extravagant is our welcome to those who sit as the minority in the room, who seek to be a part of the body of Christ without abandoning their voice, their identity, their narratives, or their experiences? Are we calling for our children, youth, and their families to come as they are, or are we asking them to check their race, orientation, identities, and suffering at the door?

Are we asking the suffering and the oppressed to choose between Black Lives Matter and the church; Open and Affirming and the church; immigration and the church; or gender equality and the church? These issues impact the communities, the cultures, the homes, the schools and classrooms, the hospitals, the access to food and water, and the ability to live a life that is whole and free. We must engage these issues and remain on the ball, lest we become bench warmers watching and wait-ing and signifying as witnesses for Christ.

This is a *kairos* moment for the church to be prophetic in witness and works. That is the prayerful hope of summertime.

Summertime is the time for the prophetic works of social justice to manifest themselves, because it means we have been doing the labour, planting the seeds, being faithful in our harvest year-round. It is not a time to take the work for granted or to slumber. We must remain vigilant, because Ella Baker said,

> *We who believe in freedom cannot rest until it comes*
> *Until the killing of Black men and Black mothers' sons*
> *is as important as the killing of White men and White mothers' sons...*
> *We who believe in freedom cannot rest until it comes...*[5]

The church can no longer be comfortable in the sanctuary. The witness of our denominations must go beyond creating press releases and resolutions and trending social media sites and web pages just for the sake of attracting youth to come and hold down the pews while we don't give a damn about the suffering, oppression, and traumatizing realities that are inundating them, their peers, and their communities day in and day out, season after season. There is no rest for our children in the summertime!

The church leaders, our youth leaders, every member of our faith community – the village of a beloved community – must be authentic, intentional, and actively engaged members of the community in which we serve in order to be that expectant hope.

Philando Castile's murder was recorded on Facebook live. Thousands of people sat in front of their computer and smart phone screens and witnessed the man's murder, and still Black and Brown folks were told to wait, to hold on, to not protest or resist, and to not be angry! Church folks are telling people who are being slaughtered like wild animals to wait on justice and to wait on the Lord from whence cometh thy help. Wait, we say, on the Lord!

But I come to tell you that Jesus was one who disrupted the systems, turned over tables, and spoke life – not death. And Jesus was righteously angry! And if we want our children to experience the freedom and peace and joys and laughter and love and hope of summertime, we as faith leaders and communities must prophetically do the same!

To echo the words of Dr. Martin Luther King Jr., WE CAN'T WAIT!!

A bystander videotaped Walter Scott being shot five times from behind, and his murderer, also videotaped planting a weapon on Scott's lifeless body, was until recently not held accountable. The hearing was originally declared a mistrial, reminiscent of Emmett Till's killers being set free. How long must we wait?

I stand before you as a survivor of the shooting in Charleston where my first cousin, Rev. DePayne Middleton, a remarkable mother of four dynamic daughters, an unapologetic person of faith, a brilliant vocalist, and the most loyal among family and friends, was among the murdered found in the basement of Mother Emanuel late Wednesday night, June 17, 2015.

My cousin was stolen from us in the late night of summertime, during Bible study in the basement of a church, as she and eight others prayed and welcomed a stranger in their midst. They were targeted because of the colour of their skin. They were stolen from us because of a guileful false demonization of people of colour, which is too often ignored and normalized through socially-accepted practices, traditions, and symbols such as the Confederate flag, and a political climate that allows a Ku Klux Klan-endorsed candidate to ascend to the White House.

How long must we wait for summer?

People are celebrating Elizabeth Warren's persistence, but are they demonizing Black and Brown folks for their resistance? At the same time, many have forgotten that the very words Warren used to resist were the words of a Black woman whose husband was a victim of racist White Supremacy in America. This is the reality for many of our youth and their families today, and it is this reality that makes summertime a threat.

Too often we want to bypass the process of reconciliation in our efforts to do justice. Don't talk to me about forgiveness if there has not been an authentic effort to repent and call out the sin that has been brought against these stolen bodies and lives. As faith leaders we must be truth tellers. Tell the truth. The truth must be the headline. And the truth is that the deaths of these innocent lives from Chicago to Staten Island to Charleston to New Orleans to Houston expose the immorality of our nation and also the silence of those charged with moral authority – and that includes the church!

So what are we gonna do about it?

Friends, summertime is here and our children urgently need us to be who we say we are right now!

We keep telling them they are the future. So what does that make us? Are we the present? Are we the right now? Is that what we are telling them? Then how will we become the change agents and freedom fighters who are righteously angry and who resist systems of oppression right now, even if that means we must turn over tables and walk out of the pews; even if that means we must resist the norms that have been ritualized in our litanies, hymns, and worship?

We must stop looking for prophets and start being prophetic voices right now, right where we are, and with a fierce urgency of love!

This is the test of the oppressed: become their own storytellers, reclaim their stolen narratives, and share prophetic witness. Honour the voices, the narratives, and the lament. Don't silence and make invisible the pain and brokenness by pushing them to the margins – and then organize a youth group to go there. That is hypocrisy and that is a danger to the humanity of those fighting for survival.

When government and judicial systems fail to indict Pilate or the powers that be for their corruption, we must tell the truth.

When blood-stained hands have not been washed clean or expunged, we must tell the truth in order for accountability and healing and reconciliation to take place.

When people are forced to drink tainted water and risk their health and well-being, tell the truth.

When oil and profit are given greater value than people and their sacred lands, and we feel comfortable running pipelines through the graves of their ancestors (something that would never be allowed if the proposal were to run a pipeline through Arlington National Cemetery), we must tell the truth and resist.

When tear gas, rubber bullets, water hoses, and dogs are used to discourage, devalue, and disinherit God's people, we must tell the truth!

I know that most people have expectant hope in December, when we are told to celebrate the birth of Christ. But what if there was a great expectation of God's love and justice in the summertime too? What if our children could bear witness to a God who is on the side of the oppressed in every season? What if the children could expect good news in June and July and August too?

The scripture says, "You who bring good news to Jerusalem, lift up your voice with a shout, lift it up, do not be afraid; say to the towns of Judah, 'Here is your God!'" (Is 40:9 NIV).

Let us show our children, "Here is your God!" by our examples, our righteous anger and resistance, and our authentic worship and works. It must go beyond the scriptures and become our service.

We are the repairers of the breach. This is our work.

This is our duty.

This is our responsibility.

And it is the right of our children to feel the sun, to know the freedoms of summer, and to know God's love, because God's love lives through and through every sector of their lives. If they don't know it anywhere else, my God, let them know it from the church!

Let them know it from their youth leaders and their pastors and denominational leaders!

Let them see God in us, because each day they so sweetly and generously show us the God in them. If they can give so generously, why can't we? Why won't we? When will we be the sun rays they seek? When will we be the shade so many desperately need? When will we be the cool waters? When will we be their rock and their strength?

Here are the names of the stolen. They are ours. They were beloved created beings, stolen too soon.

Sandra Bland
Rekia Boyd
Ralkina Jones
LaQuan Mcdonald, 16 years old and shot 16 times,
one bullet for every year of his life
Freddie Gray
Tamir Rice
Tanisha Anderson
Jordan Davis
Michael Brown
Trayvon Martin
Sarah Lee Circle Bear
Miriam Carey

These are the narratives of the oppressed.

They did not seek the warmth of other suns. They sought the warmth of the suns in their own neighbourhoods, homes, communities, and nation, and their lives were eclipsed much like the sun is eclipsed.

Let the church be like a gurgling spring and a well-watered garden so that when those who thirst see us, they will know it is not a mirage, but living water.

Let us offer prayers rooted in works and not in rituals that run dry.

Let us be a powerful force rolling on like a river, righteous like a never-failing stream.

Let us dare to tell the truth! We must declare Black lives matter until it is true.

Let us tell the truth. The whole truth and nothing but the truth, so help us God!

Don't look away.

Don't ignore the cries.

Don't discard the narratives of your neighbours.

Don't presume that the sun shining through your windows can reach the hidden places in the margins where there are those who are unable to even fathom a sunrise.

In the revolutionary era of the 1960s when antiwar songs invigorated grassroots movements, Pete Seeger wrote the folk song, "Where Have All the Flowers Gone?" What a great question for those seeking the evidence of summertime.

While that query is still relevant today, Dr. Marvin McMickle notes that there is yet still a homiletical equivalent to that question, which asks, "Where have all the prophets gone?"[6]

Where have all the prophets gone?
Gone in search of mega-churches, every one.
Where have all the prophets gone?
Gone in search of faith-based funding, every one.
Where have all the prophets gone?
Gone in search of personal comfort, every one.
Where have all the prophets gone?
Gone in search of political correctness, every one.
Where have all the prophets gone?
Gone into a ministry that places praise over speaking truth to power,
every one.
When will they ever learn? When will they ever learn?[7]

We have been here before. We have heard the wild and disorderly voice of one calling in the wilderness, "Make straight the way of the Lord" (Jn 1:23). But did those Pharisees listen to John? Did those disciples listen to those women running to bear witness to truth from the tomb? Did we listen to those children and youth on the streets in Birmingham during the Civil Rights movement; are we listening to the children and youth on the streets in Ferguson and Chicago in this era of movement and resistance right now? When will we listen? When will we learn? Sometimes the ministers are not in the pulpit. Perhaps they are the unchurched, the uncalled, the resistors we thought we came to teach. Perhaps we leaders, ministers, and teachers are also here to learn.

"Summertime" used to be a lullaby of hope. What say you this day? Dare we sing a song of hope?

Summertime, and the livin' is easy
Fish are jumpin' and the cotton is high
Oh, your daddy's rich and your ma is good-lookin'
So hush, little baby, don't you cry
One of these mornings you're gonna rise up singing
And you'll spread your wings and you'll take to the sky
But till that morning, there ain't nothin' can harm you
With daddy and mammy standin' by
One of these mornings you're gonna rise up singing
And you'll spread your wings and you'll take to the sky!

Singing,
Until that morning comes, we got a lot of work to do.
Until that morning comes, we got a lot of work to do.

1. DuBose Heyward, *Summertime*. Lyrics: https://genius.com.
2. African-American spiritual.
3. Abel Meeropol, *Strange Fruit*. (New York, NY: Edward B. Marks Music Company).
4. Toni Morrison, *Beloved* (New York: Knopf, 1987/2006), 103.
5. Ella Baker, *Ella's Song* Dr. Bernice Johnson Reagon, https://ellabakercenter.org
6. Marvin McMickle, *Where Have All the Prophets Gone? Reclaiming Prophetic Preaching in America* (Cleveland: Pilgrim, 2006), Kindle location 176-187.
7. Ibid.

4.

Make Youth Ministry Great Again

Disrupting White Supremacy in the Age of Donald Trump and Michael Brown

DANIEL WHITE HODGE

Daniel White Hodge, PhD, is a recognized urban youth culture expert and cultural literacy scholar. He is Associate Professor of Intercultural Communications and department chair of Communication Arts at North Park University in Chicago. His research interests are the intersections of faith, hip hop culture, race/ethnicity, and young adult emerging generations.
www.whitehodge.com.

A Personal Introduction to the Post-Civil Rights Era

We were sitting in my fourth-period English class during my senior year in high school; Mrs. Williamson, if I remember correctly. About a month prior, the school had installed a closed-circuit television in the classroom. It just so happened that we had been discussing the power of speech that day, and the TV was on as we awaited a very important verdict. The time in class was spent as I normally spent it at 18 years old – doing as little as possible and waiting for the class to end so that I could hang with my friends. A group of us were zoning in and out as Mrs. Williamson gave out instructions. Then the room got silent. The jury was about to give its verdict. One by one, the judge asked each juror for their verdict, and, one by one, the response was "not guilty."

Not *guilty*? Did they see the tape of Stacey Koon, Laurence Powell, Theodore Briseno, and Timothy Wind savagely beating Rodney King? Maybe the tape was too blurry for them. *Not* guilty? Was this really happening?

Rage filled my mind. Acid poured into my gut. Half the class got up and walked out of the room. Mrs. Williamson attempted to stop us – class was not over – but it was a moot effort. This was too much to take sitting down.

We took our rage, anger, sadness, and feelings of betrayal by a system that had too long favoured White males outside. In a haze of confusion, we yelled, debated; some even wept. My friend Larry pulled out an American flag and began to burn it. We all cheered. Within a matter of ten minutes, there were at least 1,200 students gathered outside in the central part of campus. *Not guilty*? For years, we in the Black and urban community had endured beatings. Police would take us down to the wharf because the sea lions there made a tremendous amount of noise and no one would hear us if we yelled as they savagely beat us. For years, I saw friends of mine die from blunt force trauma to the head because some police officer assumed they were resisting arrest. For years, we saw Black and multi-ethnic young women sexually abused, sexually harassed, and, in some cases, raped by police officers. No officers were ever arrested, brought to trial, or even investigated. When we attempted to take these accusations to someone, we ourselves were arrested, laughed at, or told "you probably deserved it." Not guilty?

Yes, Rodney King had charged the officers when they finally pulled him over – the now infamous video footage has edited that out. Yes, Rodney King was drunk, speeding, and did not pull over when the officers requested he do so. But April 29, 1992 was about much more than King's infractions. Did King deserve to be beaten, for that long, with that ferocity, after he was already on the ground and subdued? No.

What ensued was one of the greatest civil unrests of the 20th century, and it began on that warm, late-April afternoon in 1992. I was a part of those uprisings. I openly participated in the push-back, and I was ready to die for equality and my humanity. As a young, Black, militant, frustrated male, I had had enough. Hundreds of us had reached our limits of patience waiting for the "system" to give us "justice." Not guilty. Yes. That was the verdict.

I recall my youth pastor at the time being just as angry. Caught between his religion and the realities of the youth in his ministry, he decided to remain at church, praying with others. I respected his decision to stay and pray at the time, and I still respect it. But he was caught; caught between what he knew to be true regarding the history of police brutality and violent force toward Black youth, and a Christianity that told him to "turn the other cheek."[1] Caught between wanting to act on the issues and what he felt his faith was leading him to do.

Now, a theology of violence is neither what I am arguing for here nor my point. My thought here is to hold in tension a Christian theology that seems to act viciously, say, in the face of "injustice" concerning unborn children and abortion, yet is often not able to extend that same voraciousness toward lives lost in urban communities or the injustices that befall them. A Christian theology that overwhelmingly approves a "war" with Iraq, yet continues to remain silent on issues such as the effects of the prison industrial complex on urban America, or the reality of what the "war on drugs" has done to urban multi-ethnic communities.[2] And a Christian theology that overwhelmingly voted for a known racist, xenophobic, sexist human being for president.

Fast forward to July of 2014, and the Michael Brown murder in Ferguson. Once again, the flames of racial injustice sparked up. Once more, uprisings occurred, and the debate on race was at an all-time high. What do you do as a youth pastor? What do you as a Christian? Do you remain silent? Do you just "pray about" the situation and send "prayers and thoughts"? How do you react when you see, on the media, "riots" and people "looting"? Do you shake your head in disgust? Look the other way? Accuse the police officers involved? How does the gospel fit into all of this? Would Jesus be standing on the sidelines and "just praying" about the situation? How might we, as a church community, do youth ministry in a setting like this? Given the events, not only in Ferguson but around the country, how does race affect *your* youth ministry, especially in the era of Trump? How do students react when someone of a different ethnic background enters the room? How do the events of the Zoot Suit Riots affect your students, historically?

Disturbing Comfortable Youth Ministry

In Matthew 28, we see a narrative we all know: the Great Commission. Many of us read that and assume it is a calling to "go forth" and "preach the gospel." In one regard it is. Yet, in other regards, it requires us to be uncomfortable and to move beyond the zones of Christianese that we inhabit during Sunday morning totemic gatherings. This passage contains grey-matter certitude: Verse 17 says, "When they saw him, they worshiped him; *but some doubted.*" This is important to remember, but we forget this and quickly move on.

The time of Jesus was not a "simple time." Death, corruption, heinous crime, and lawlessness were throughout the land.[3] Moreover, many doubted that this was Jesus to begin with. *Why are we even worshipping this dude? He could be an imposter.* Sounds like a familiar cabin time talk with students. Doubt: an essential part of faith development for both the youth minister and student. Doubt, as R.T. France puts it, "...denotes a state of uncertainty and hesitation" within the disciples.[4]

Yet, in the blend of that doubt, Jesus does not miss a beat. He picks right up and issues out the Great Commission, and uses a word that sets the tone for this chapter: *ethnos.* In verse 19 Jesus says, "Therefore go and make disciples of all nations..." That word "nations" is from the Greek *ethnos* and is where we get the word "ethnicity" from. *Ethnos* primarily deals with ethnic "cultural" aspects and is concerned with different "tribes." Jesus uses it here to emphasize that his message was to be taken to people who were specifically "foreign," "out there," and different – meaning non-Jewish, pagan, Gentile, heathen, from diverse nations and/or different people groups.[5]

This is a powerful statement from Jesus, made not just to his disciples, but vicariously through the disciples to us as well. In this vortex, we can begin our discussion on race, because at the centre of this vortex lies the heart of the gospel: love, reconciliation, self-consciousness/awareness, and action. In addition, the messier life gets, the more room, time, and space the gospel has to actually do its job. The neater we try to make it, the worse it gets. In other words, if we ignore, haphazardly repair, or remain silent about it, racism will continue to grow and thrive. Jesus is pointing us to his word and to community in him and with others. We have to remember: the gospel comforts the disturbed and disturbs the comforted.

Therefore, and especially as we take into account the election year of 2016, this chapter is primarily about disturbing the comforted; the comforted being White Supremacy and White Christianity. This chapter will assert the necessity for youth workers[6] to deal with race in an era of Trump, Michael Brown, Trayvon Martin, Freddie Gray, and the countless other young Black and multiethnic lives that have been lost over the years at the hands of racism. It is our duty as youth pastors, workers, and ministers to "get in" and do something beyond "prayers and warm thoughts." The Christian suburban fortresses and the sacred canopies of private Christian colleges can no longer remain "in prayer." The time for action is now! The Gospel demands it. In our doubt, in our faith, in our worship, Jesus calls us to the *ethnos*. Jesus calls us to commune with students and others who rise up in Los Angeles, Ferguson, New York City, Iraq, Syria, Palestine, and who desire a better world.

I feel it necessary to explain the reasons for writing this chapter. First, youth ministry is dominated by White cisgender male American voices. While many in the youth ministry world would agree with that, there has yet to be a significant shift toward creating space for ethnic minority youth ministry voices, particularly in the realm of Christian publishing. While there are networks such as Urban Youth Workers Institute (UYWI) and Christian Community Development Association (CCDA), their voices are still at the margins of Christian youth ministry.[7] Hence, issues such as race, gender, and class are not well engaged throughout the youth ministry literature. Further, the silence from the White evangelical church in the wake of the Charleston terrorist attacks and the ensuing burning of Black churches has been resounding. This silence was broken, however, when Donald J. Trump entered the

Republican presidential race and an overwhelming 81% of White evangelicals voted for him on the heels of a Black president.

Second, issues such as White racism[8] continue to be on the agenda at staple youth ministry events such as camping and mission trips, and in youth groups that are less homogeneous in nature. In these environments, micro-aggression is normal, and the significance of race lingers as a factor in deciding what music is played, who is "helping" whom (in the context of short-term missions), and whose cultural norms are standardized as "right." Additionally, the messages received about who is in charge centre on Whiteness. These factors hinder the gospel and ministry. Once again, Traci West reminds us that a gospel and a Christology focused on and rooted in Whiteness create a sense of superiority and power detrimental to youth ministry, while serving to place one race over the other.[9] And as Karen Teel puts it, "Whiteness can today be defined as a system of hegemonic power that operates to benefit people perceived to be White and to disadvantage people perceived to be of color."[10] Thus, it is critical in a post-civil rights context that we begin to move past this existing hegemony in youth ministry into one that reflects the current demographic and cultural changes happening in North America.

I will now outline two crucial motifs that must be engaged in this era of socio-theological unrest in order to push past a White Supremacist stance in youth ministry. Let us begin.

Beyond the Great White Hero

As has been previously stated, one of the challenges to youth ministry is that it is dominated by White, upper middle class, male American norms. More important is that this must change moving forward. While Kara Powell, Andy Root, Mark Oestreicher, Doug Fields, David Lynn, Mark Matlock, Jonathan McKee, Duffy Robbins, Rick Lawrence, Jim Candy, and Chap Clark all provide excellent research, theology, and resource material for youth ministers, and should continue to do so, we are not moving toward a White, suburban, affluent world. The United States is multi-ethnic, intercultural, and diverse, and so are many other countries. Youth ministry must include perspectives from ethnic minorities, from women from a variety of ethnic backgrounds, and from voices in and within the margins. Where is the Indigenous voice? Why aren't more Black, Latino, Asian, or Pacific Islander peoples writing resources for youth ministers? Are old White men the only ones who can write commentaries and texts, and create neat-nice corners on Western theology?"[11]

Soong-Chan Rah tells us that, "Because theology emerging from a Western, White context is considered normative, it places non-Western theology in an inferior position and elevates Western theology as the standard by which all other theological frameworks and points of view are measured."[12] Such is the case with youth ministry resources and scholarship. When research is presented, it is as if it reflects a sum total of youth rather than just a sample; a summative approach that "all youth" are "this way" so that power remains with a White Western approach to youth ministry. Rah says, "This bias stifles the theological dialogue between various cultures."[13] And it most certainly stifles youth ministry dialogue about how youth culture, the gospel, and culture relate and connect from diverse perspectives – not just a White one.

Youth ministry is held captive by White suburban theology that does not allow for a multi-ethnic perspective on youth culture, and that maintains power for White theologians and youth ministers.[14] Peter Nash confirms that "attendant assumptions of a racial hierarchy that assumes the intellectual and moral superiority of the Caucasians have hampered our understanding of the text by unnecessarily eliminating possible avenues of study."[15] White theological approaches to youth ministry become the closest to God and the ones youth pastors refer to as *the* central resource. Nash once again confirms that "it is a pretentious illusion that there is something pure and objective about the way theology has been done in the Western church, as if it were handed down directly by the Almighty to the theologians of the correct methodology."[16]

This type of theological captivity and construction echoes what William R. Jones calls *divine racism*.[17] While I do not necessarily believe any current White theologians are arguing for a God that is adherently and directly against Black-skinned or ethnic minority people (although with the rise of the Alt-Right more disturbing literature is emerging giving evidence to that), the implications of a continual stream of literature featuring a White deity and White Bible characters suggest that the message remains the same: God, and Christianity in turn, must be White. Therefore, if Whites have created hegemony of power and racism, does it not stand to reason that God would in turn have a racist bent? Many ethnic minority youth are asking this complex, yet very real, question.[18]

Further, Whiteness is always given preferential treatment in almost every space. At camp, for example, a week might be termed "urban" or "multicultural," yet the worship style, pedagogy, and theological premise remain White. To add, when multi-ethnic youth do want some representation from the front stage or in the events, it can be met with resistance so as to not "offend" or "upset" White campers. And the strong voice of multi-ethnics in response to oppression and inequality is almost always eliminated when it comes to protecting White donors. Whiteness in many youth ministry settings is therefore coddled and cared for over multi-ethnic pursuits. The standard example of this is when there are "too many" multi-ethnic faces in a publication. Some Whites have problems with that and call it "reverse racism." Yet when there are homogenous images, the claim that there is preference to Whiteness is typically ignored. This continued deference to Whiteness must be eradicated if a true post-civil rights youth ministry is to be achieved.

In my own research, when young adult interviewees were asked to describe God or Jesus, all but four of them offered up images that were White. Could this be the result of years of religious socialization? Possibly, but the deeper implication is that clearly a message of power is being put forth that holds that God is a White God and Christianity is a White religion.[19] This is difficult for many post-civil rights youth, including White socially conscious ones, to accept. The research I have conducted, while not suggesting young people are "walking away from God," does suggest that they will either create new and contextual spaces for finding a God who is racially and ethnically relatable or leave Christianity in search of faiths that present a multi-ethnic deity – or at least one that is not representative of an oppressor.

We must push past this and prophetically speak against racism in all areas of society. Therefore, what follows here are suggestions based on my life as a Black male, my work in youth ministry circles for two decades, and my research performed on and in the field of youth ministry. These suggestions do not constitute a "fix all" Western approach to becoming non-racist overnight; *fixing* the problem sometimes seems more desirable than *dealing* with it. These suggestions are for White/Euro-American youth ministry contexts with an influx or growth of ethnic minorities to their population. Further, they are for the White/Euro-American youth ministry that is attempting to navigate the often sensitive area of race relations within urban/suburban contexts. These suggestions are to aid in pushing past and dealing with good intentions, tokenism, racial ignorance, and paternalism so that the widening gulf between White/Euro-Americans and ethnic minorities can be reduced, and so that we move beyond White dominant captivity of youth ministry theology.

Beyond Good Intentions

First, *good intentions never work*. Good intentions are what they are – just good intentions. While the *intention* of the situation may be noble, may be righteous, may be principled, it is the *effect* that makes all the difference. People may arrive at a space where they feel they are doing a "good" work for the ethnic minority community of young people they are working among, yet if they don't know the real needs of the community, they perpetuate neo-colonialism in that setting.[20] Particularly so if the leadership of the church is not willing to have leaders from that ethnic minority population hold positions of power and influence. The intentions of the leader may themselves be biblical; yet without both willingness to surrender their own ethnic power and better understanding of their own race and ethnic identity, all that will happen is that the leader's frame of reference, which will be

Western and non-contextual for the ethnic minority student, will be replicated. This perpetuates a White colonial model of ministry and an actual captivity of the gospel by what are deemed "right" and "acceptable" forms of doing ministry and theology. This is especially the case when researchers suggest that "all youth" are losing their faith after high school,[21] and that a generation of "nones"[22] is in a decline in faith. While true for a portion of youth, urban and multi-ethnic youth are reimagining what their spirituality might be. And while they are questioning the traditions of the past, as this book has illustrated and argued, they are not just "losing their faith" in a secular gnostic society.

Once again, good intentions. The research overall is good. But it does not apply to everyone, and a more robust and diverse set of research is needed. Good intentions within youth ministry and approaching, say, short-term missions, can do more harm than good. "I didn't mean to say it that way," or the classic "That's not what I meant," are just not enough to create a lasting intercultural engagement. Further, White people cannot go on living in their mistakes, shortcomings, and ignorance of multi-ethnic experiences. To do so is to assume the role of a racist, and one that is not willing to move beyond one's own ethnic illiteracy and unawareness of other cultures. The *impact* always outweighs the *intent*.

Beyond the Great White Hope

Second, *move beyond the great White hope mentality.* This mentality is a paralyzing one for ethnic minorities because it places White/Euro-Americans above "them" and over the context in a position of power. Privileged and racially-unconscious White/Euro-Americans tend to have a stance of power and domination; that of a conqueror.[23] Hence, it stands to reason that this attitude and personality carries itself into ministry settings, especially ones in which there is a "hero" role to be filled. While this role is not limited to the White/Euro-American ethnic group, it can be aggravated when the "hope" becomes that of a White, male, seminary-educated, heterosexual leader to "save" "those people" from whatever is defined as sin. Moreover, when key positions in ministry are not reflective of the community that they are serving, then, once again, neo-colonialism is taking place and the great White hope is squarely placed on White leadership.

A renowned urban ministry in southern California has been active in the Hollywood area for almost two decades. They perform good work and have gained national attention. Yet their senior leadership is principally White/Euro-American in a context that is predominantly Black, Latino, and Asian. This is an example of the great White hope in action: "we," meaning the White/Euro-American leadership, will "save" you. The grip on power remains in the hands of individuals who do not reflect the community context.[24]

Empowerment is crucial in the urban post-civil rights youth ministry context. When the senior leadership remains White, it suggests that we, the White power structure, do not trust you, the ethnic minorities, to present the gospel or even run an organization, and we know best. This continues the vicious legacy of racism and neo-urban colonialism, in which Whites are in control, maintain a racial habitus, and continue to promote a White Western gospel to ethnic minorities.[25] Youth ministry is not served well in this paralyzing habitus that creates a context in which White is always best, right, and theologically accurate.[26]

Beyond White Jesus

Third, and lastly, *we serve a multi-ethnic Jesus.* For many years, urban youth, hip hoppers, Blacks, and society in general have had to deal with an image foreign to them – the face of a White, blonde, blue-eyed Jesus. James Cone argued that there needed to be an image of a Jesus that was both relational and racially-appealing to people: one that ethnic minorities in the United States could adjoin to; one that was socially aware of the issues that Blacks, Latinos, and all non-dominant groups had to struggle with; one that would show compassion for them because of their hardships.[27]

Rap artist[28] and ghetto mystic Tupac Shakur took the ideology of the Black Jesus a step further and talked about a Christ figure for the ghetto. This was a Christ who smoked weed, drank liquor, kicked it, and had compassion for the 'hood; a Christ who was a human link to deity, the literal image of the Christ – God incarnate. This is a difficult image of Jesus. This is not the traditional form of Jesus, either literally or figuratively. For many traditional Christians, this image was simply too irreverent and sacrilegious. Yet this is a contextualized and appropriate theological discourse in making a God more relatable for a people group. The image of the Black Jesus was one that could connect with the downtrodden. Jesus, even as the opening chapter in Matthew reveals, was a multi-ethnic Messiah. His lineage is an example of the diversity within the saviour we serve; therefore our ministries should reflect that diversity.[29]

Sobering Up

There is much work before us, and the rise of ethnic minority students within White/Euro-American suburban contexts is growing.[30] Soong-Chan Rah prompts us to remember this:

> *We face a challenging reality. We live under the reality of the oppression of the Western, White captivity of the church. We may claim that our version of evangelicalism [or another form of Christianity] is culture-free, that we are merely trying to be culturally relevant, or that we are trying to maintain the church's tradition, and thereby ultimately reject the claim of cultural captivity. But the reality of the situation is that Western, White culture dominates American culture and, in turn, dominates American evangelicalism*[31]

A sobering reality that Rah challenges us to move past.

This chapter does not fully address the issues of intercultural communication, diversity competencies, gender, and diverse ministry settings. All these areas are valid and need their own attention, especially in the era we find ourselves in within North America and the Western world at large. The issue of how best to serve violent teens entering a seemingly "calm" and serene suburban church setting is growing as well.[32] Thus, it is imperative that we return continually to the mandate in Matthew 28 to introspectively examine our approach to the *ethnos* – those who are different from us. These issues constitute just a fraction of the ongoing racism in the United States, and we as Christians and youth ministers must address them in order to limit the damage to race relations and shape how this next generation interprets and sees God in their lives. This will bring fulfillment and more depth to youth ministry as a whole. It is messy, and it requires all of us to communicate much better, but it is part of what the gospel calls us to do as we move into that ambiguous grey area.

Now, let us focus on what moving towards a multi-ethnic approach in youth ministry might look like.

Embracing and Utilizing the Multi-Ethnic, Multi-Cultural Jesuz

I do not believe Jesus was a White, long-haired, blue-eyed, dominant culture embodiment of perfection. And yes, I do think the ethnicity of Jesus is important. To think otherwise is to follow colonialist trappings that originate in dominant culture and strip the narrative of Jesus to an abstract disembodiment of the gospel without any multi-ethnic voice. This is not the gospel. This is not our Christian heritage. Our Christian heritage, when moved beyond a Western précis, *is* complex and multicultural. Take James Cone's approach to Jesus in the context of Black suffering, which offers an opportunity to see and hear from Jesus that reaches beyond the theology of celebration that we normally hear.[33] Or take Third Eye Theology, which was formed in Asian contexts and argues for the consciousness of the mind (hence, your third eye in the mind that leads to your heart).[34] Or consider the insight Gustavo Gutierrez brings to Job that connects back the Latino experience.[35] These are all rich and diverse approaches that provide different views on what the gospel is in different regions. Further, they explore the study of Jesus, and his ministry to and for those oppressed and disenfranchised. A broader and more robust approach to Christian theology involving more female, ethnic minority, and intercultural voices will be needed in a post-civil rights era.

The traditional image of "Jesus" has been that of a bearded, White, longhaired, blue-eyed person.[36] The societal reinforcement of this image by White dominant culture has been problematic for many in the urban post-civil rights community. Therefore, a form of Christ more contextual and relevant for that context has been sought after.[37] When one takes away the domesticated and sterile symbol Jesus has become in Western Christianity, Jesus was, and still is in many ways, a controversial persona. He was not one to either mince words or miss an opportunity to connect with the disinherited. Ebony Utley discusses that.

> Jesus fraternized with sexually licentious women, cavorted with sinners, worked on the Sabbath, had a temper, used profane language with religious people, praised faithfulness over stilted forms of religious piety, and honored God more than the government. Gangstas respect Jesus because they see the parallels between his life and theirs.[38]

However, in youth ministry, most of the critical, radical, and post-soul images of Jesus have been lost or domesticated for either political or racial reasons. Post-civil rights students want to hear this controversial Jesus; they want to embrace a Jesus who is disreputable and dubious about religious folks. They want a Jesus who actually sits with the oppressed.

Is it possible that seemingly blasphemous images of the sacred Christ create spiritual awareness? Theologian Tom Beaudoin has told us that "offensive images or practices may indicate a familiarity with deep religious truths."[39] One must understand the authority of "official" sacraments to forcefully devalorize them. Likewise, it takes a true believer in the power of worship to turn curses into praise and the word "nigga" into a nomination of the highest respect. The point here is not to allow degrading terms, but to acknowledge that such rhetorical devices are making a serious theological attempt to grasp a practice of inequality that is *very* real to the people experiencing it.[40]

For example, Tupac and The Outlawz, in their song "Black Jesuz," present a Jesus who is not only relatable, but one who connects with the inequalities of life. While most of the song questions whether a Jesus is even able to connect to ethnic-minority young people, the subtext of the song is about a Jesus who can connect; a Jesus who can relieve the burden of ghetto life; a Jesus who, in the Psalmist's terms, is a shepherd who causes those in dire straits to lie down in green pastures; a Jesus who is able to blow through the blunt-smoking persona and redeem those who hurt back to him. A post-civil rights theology indeed.

These sensationalized images of Jesus are needed. More importantly, they are needed in the discourse of Christian theology and youth ministry, as many of these personas of Jesus get lost within the dominant Western Euro-American-centric Romanesque model of Christianity. Suffering in context is nothing new. The search for meaning within that suffering is nothing new. Neither is the rejection of dominant models of deity. Therefore, it should stand to reason that Hip Hop artists such as Tupac, Kendrick Lamar, Lauryn Hill, Propagana, Lecrae, Odd Thomas, and Pastor Troy create the post-soul space in which to dissect a much more multifaceted and compound image of Jesus: a Jesus who can relate, a Jesus so contextual that we must change the last letter of his name to "z."

The z represents us. It represents a version of God not heard: a God from the margins and the disenfranchised. The multi-ethnic Jesus adds the z at the end of the name to illustrate the difference in context, locality, habitus, and theological stance, and to signify the change. This is not done in blasphemy nor out of disrespect for Christ. In fact, quite the opposite; the letter z at the end of Jesus' name adds post-civil rights validity by portraying a Jesus who can sympathize and connect with a people who are downtrodden and broken. White, Black, Asian, Latino, and Native peoples can all connect with that, as pain and suffering are universal. The z represents a Jesus who is not only *above* in theological requisitions, but also *below* in accessible form. The new dimensions given by the z to the portrait of Christ validate the struggles, lives, narratives, and spirituality of many youth living in a post-civil rights and post-soul context. This is the Jesus of history, I believe, and this Jesus would be foreign to many churches today because of his robust and gregarious approach to organized religion.[41]

Sensationalized images of Jesus, such as Aaron McGruder's Black Jesus, Lil Wayne's Trap Jesus, and Tupac's Black Jesuz, represent a fundamental attempt to make deity, the divine, and the sacred more accessible to those who typically do not grace the sanctuaries of Christian churches and youth ministries. They represent the fusing of the profane with the sacred – that vortex we have been discussing. They use culture to help interpret the sacred scriptures, and humour to break away some of the seriousness characteristically associated with Jesus. They are more relevant and applicable to those seeking Jesus from the post-soul, hip hop, and post-civil rights generation. This generation is not interested in a God that sits in multi-million dollar churches on high, disconnected from any suffering and pain; a God that desires only a theology of celebration and avoids a theology of suffering. This generation rejects pastors who net more than all their congregations make in a year combined. They despise the double standards of the church, and they do not want a Jesus who is "too perfect." A multi-ethnic and multi-cultural approach to Jesus is what's needed in our youth ministries now. It is time for a multi-ethnic Jesuz! Because, as James Cone so firmly reminds us,

...Jesus' death was a sacrifice. Thus the reality and the depth of God's presence in human suffering are revealed not only in Jesus' active struggle against suffering during his ministry but especially in his death on the cross. The cross of Jesus reveals the extent of God's involvement in the suffering of the weak. God is not merely sympathetic with the social pain of the poor but becomes totally identified with them in their agony and pain. The pain of the oppressed is God's pain, for God takes their suffering as God's own, thereby freeing them from its ultimate control of their lives. The oppressed do not have to worry about suffering because its power over their lives was defeated

by God. God in Christ became the Suffering Servant and thus took the humiliation and suffering of the oppressed into God's own history.[42]

This is about bringing disruption to White Supremacy within youth ministry. In an era of Trump, the time to act is now. It is not the moment to stay still or silent. Silence sides with the oppressor. And part of what Western Christianity has done is to paralyze the action that we as Christians should take in the face of hate and White racism. Jesus did not stand still. He did not offer up "warm thoughts" for the people he healed or dealt with. Jesus was a radical. It is time we embrace that radical nature in order to combat White racism. We need a framework that takes us toward a context of "missionary approaching a post-civil rights youth culture."

This chapter is not here to answer all of your questions. Rather, I want to disturb you just enough to take a closer look at some serious issues facing the Christian faith. No one book can do that. And, like I tell my students in all of my classes, if I have helped you critically look at the material, you will leave with more questions than you have answers – and that is always a good thing! Let us carry on, missionally, into a post-civil rights youth ministry.

1. While this chapter does not allow the space to discuss the concept of "divine racism" as postulated by William Jones, it is noted that a growing number of emerging adults in the post-civil rights generation regard Black Christianity as an oppressive theology because it was given to Blacks from White slavers and thereby is still rooted in White racism. This is a growing trend among some Black post-civil rights youth under 18 who, because of the age of information, have a much wider access to data sets and as a result have critically engaged Christian theology. They assert that many ethnic minorities (not just Blacks) are simply following a religion created to brainwash them into "peace" and "forgiveness," while Whites, the oppressors, utilize violence for religious justifications anytime they please. See William R. Jones, *Is God a White Racist? A Preamble to Black Theology* (Garden City, NY: Anchor, 1973). To add, it is as Traci West has asserted: "When missionaries who converted enslaved blacks in the Americas or colonized in

Africa taught a Christology informed by White dominance-Black inferiority mythology, their evangelism confused truth with lies." Traci C. West, "When a White Man-God Is the Truth and the Way for Black Christians," in *Christology and Whiteness: What Would Jesus Do?*, edited by George Yancy, 114-27. (New York: Routledge, 2012), 115.

2. For some scholars, the "war on drugs" is a war on the urban communities. Moreover, it is a war on Black people. The "war on drugs" is a vernacular that does not hold true to its mission – to eradicate illegal drugs and the usage of them. This "war" has resulted in many being sent to prison for drug use and an even wider gap between the actual entry point of said drugs and the distributors of that drug, who are often low-level individuals who live in impoverished conditions. Thus, the ideology surrounding the "war on drugs" becomes a farce for some, as it has little to do with an actual process of getting rid of the drugs and is often used as a means to imprison a people group. See Michelle Alexander, *The New Jim Crow: Mass Incarceration in the Age of Colorblindness* (New York: The New Press, 2010), and United States, Congress, Senate, Committee on Governmental Affairs, and Permanent Subcommittee on Investigations, *Drugs and Violence: The Criminal Justice System in Crisis: Hearings before the Permanent Subcommittee on Investigations of the Committee on Governmental Affairs, United States Senate, One Hundred First Congress, First Session, June 26, 1989 (Macon, Ga) and June 28, 1989 (Atlanta, Ga)* [in English] (Washington: U.S. G.P.O.: For sale by the Supt. of Docs., Congressional Sales Office, U.S. G.P.O., 1989).

3. Robert Walter Funk, Roy W. Hoover, and The Jesus Seminar, *The Five Gospels: What Did Jesus Really Say?* (San Francisco: HarperSanFrancisco, 1993/1997), 6-9.

4. R. T. France, *Tyndale New Testament Commentaries: Matthew* (Grand Rapids: IVP Academic, 1985), 412.

5. Taken from Strong's Greek & Hebrew Dictionary on the word Ethnos (1486).

6. By writing this chapter with an eye for youth ministry, I also recognize that much of what I write also applies to those who work primarily with children.

7. Yet the glamor and novelty of urban/social-justice work is rising among many evangelical circles. With emerging conferences such as "The Justice Conference" (in which the senior leadership remains White), a growing trend is to mention discourses such as justice or equality and therefore create a "new" type of market for White Gen Ys/Millennials who tend to have a stronger bend toward issues surrounding justice. What the outcome of this will be, and whether or not

these startups will pay homage to urban greats such as John Perkins, Lina Thompson, Rene Rochester, and many others, still remains to be seen.

8. White racism is a framework used by many critical race theorists. See, for example, Terrace Crawford, *Going Social: A Practical Guide on Social Media for Church Leaders* (Kansas City, MO: Beacon Hill, 2012); George Yancy, ed. *Christology and Whiteness: What Would Jesus Do?* (New York: Routledge, 2012); William H. Watkins, *The White Architects of Black Education: Ideology and Power in America, 1865-1954* (New York: Teachers College Press, 2001); Cornel West, *Race Matters* (Boston: Beacon, 1993); Eduardo Bonilla-Silva, *Racism Without Racists: Color-Blind Racism and the Persistence of Racial Inequality in America*, 5th ed. (Lanham, MD: Rowman and Littlefield, 2018); Eduardo Bonilla-Silva, *White Supremacy and Racism in the Post-Civil Rights Era* (Boulder, CO: L. Rienner, 2001), which specifically draw attention to racism in and among Whites and White culture. White racism is a framework necessary here because it situates Whiteness in Christianity and creates a specific conversation around racism and White people - something missing from many Christian texts.

9. West, "When a White Man-God Is the Truth and the Way for Black Christians," 116-22.

10. Karen Teel, "What Jesus Wouldn't Do: A White Theologian Engages Whiteness," in *Christology and Whiteness: What Would Jesus Do?* edited by George Yancy, 19-35 (New York: Routledge, 2012), 20.

11. While many of the sources used to support this argument are from the social sciences and critical race theory fields, this does not negate the fact that there are great youth ministry authors doing good work in our field. Yet the majority of texts on youth ministry do not take into account the significance and continuing issue of race. Therefore, the sources used in order to create a new space for discussions regarding race/ethnicity in youth ministry come from outside the field of youth ministry.

12. Soong-Chan Rah, *The Next Evangelicalism: Freeing the Church from Western Cultural Captivity* (Downers Grove, IL: InterVarsity, 2009), 78.

13. Ibid.

14. George Yancy, "Introduction: Facing the Problem," in *Christology and Whiteness: What Would Jesus Do?*, edited by George Yancy, 1-18 (New York: Routledge, 2012).

15. Peter T. Nash, *Reading Race, Reading the Bible* (Minneapolis: Fortress, 2003), 58.

16. Nash, *Reading Race*, 25, 26.

17. In this, Jones contends, "The first distinctive trait of divine racism to be noted is its appeal to a 'two-category system'; it

presupposes a basic division of mankind [*sic*] into an 'in' group and an 'out' group. In addition, this fundamental division is supported, initiated, or sanctioned by God Himself. God has special concern for the 'in' group, and it receives His sustaining aid and grace. By contrast, He is indifferent or hostile to the 'out' group. In sum, God does not value all men equally; consequently, He treats them differently. And this difference is not accidental but central to His will and purpose." Jones, *Is God a White Racist?*, 244-46.

18. This question was wrestled with in my research among hip hoppers and their spirituality. The theme of God and God's race continually arose. Artists like Tupac become prophetic when they ask, "Is God another racist White cop waiting to beat my ass?" This is crucial for us as youth ministers to hold in tension, wrestle with, and eventually answer. Daniel White Hodge, *Hip Hop's Hostile Gospel: A Post-Soul Theological Exploration* (Boston: Brill Academic, 2016).

19. This particular argument is similar to the one that many African Americans had at the onset of the ending of slavery. Was Christianity the "master's" religion? Was there room for Blacks in the faith? It had been used for centuries in favour of slavery, so it must be a racist religion. See Darlene Clark Hine, William C Hine, and Stanley Harrold, *The African American Odyssey*, Vol. 1, 4th ed. (Upper Saddle River, NJ: Prentice Hall, 2010). This argument continues today in the face of extreme racism in the United States. Many young people I talk with are struggling to find Christianity contextually appropriate and even a faith that is active in the face of injustice and evil. Given that the U.S. portrays Christianity as a conservative, evangelical, rigid religion, the odds are that many ethnic-minority youth living in post-civil rights contexts will leave the faith to seek out more relatable faiths.

20. Several scholars have addressed the issue of neo-colonialism in the Christian ministry setting. See Roy L. Brooks, *Racial Justice in the Age of Obama* (Princeton: Princeton University Press, 2009); J. Kameron Carter, *Race: A Theological Account* (New York: Oxford University Press, 2008); James H. Cone, *The Cross and the Lynching Tree* (Maryknoll, NY: Orbis, 2011); James E. Evans, *We Have Been Believers: An African American Systematic Theology* (Minneapolis: Fortress, 1992); Rah, *The Next Evangelicalism*. This issue is exacerbated when the White/Euro-American youth worker approaches the ministry table believing they "know" more and can "teach" "these people" something similar to the leaders of the organization in the opening story of this article – an attitude sometimes found in White/Euro-American missionaries (Rah, *The Next Evangelicalism*, 76-80).

21. As with the Sticky Faith campaign, which asserts a notion that students lose their faith after leaving youth group.See Kara E. Powell, Brad M. Griffin, and Cheryl A. Crawford, *Sticky Faith, Youth Worker Edition: Practical Ideas to Nurture Long-Term Faith in Teenagers* (Grand Rapids: Zondervan, 2011), 16-25. While this may be true for some, this is clearly not the case for many Black students who go to college and actually remain in a faith community, as I have found in my own research. See Daniel White Hodge, *Heaven Has a Ghetto: The Missiological Gospel and Theology of Tupac Amaru Shakur* (Saarbrucken, Germany: VDM Verlag Dr. Muller Academic, 2009); Daniel White Hodge, "No Church in the Wild: Hip Hop Theology and Mission," *Missiology: An International Review* 41, no. 1 (2013): 97-109. It would be much more beneficial to suggest that this phenomenon is true for a specific set of students who are not urban, lack diversity, and are from a particular demographic.

22. Those that have no affiliation with organized religion as asserted by Gallup Poll, "In U.S., Rise in Religious 'Nones' Slows in 2012," in Gallup Poll (Gallup, 2013); Luis Logo et al., *"Nones" on the Rise: One-in-Five Adults Have No Religious Affiliation* (Washington, DC: Pew Research Center's Forum on Religion and Public Life, 2012); Barry A. Kosmin and Ariela Keysar, *American Religious Identification Survey: Summary Report* (Hartford, CT: Trinity College, 2009).

23. See Carter, *Race*; Rah, *The Next Evangelicalism*; Tim J. Wise, *Affirmative Action: Racial Preference in Black and White* (New York: Routledge, 2005); Tim Wise, *Colorblind: The Rise of Post-Racial Politics and the Retreat from Racial Equity* (San Francisco: City Lights, 2010). Also see Matthew Desmond and Mustafa Emirbayer's historical account on the social construct of Whiteness in their seminal book *Racial Domination, Racial Progress: The Sociology of Race in America* (New York: McGraw Hill, 2010), 60-63.

24. Why is this a problem? Because the people in that context have much to give and their perspective is needed to push the conversation past suburban stylized ministry. Professor Dan Shaw at Fuller Theological Seminary's School of Intercultural Studies stated that if you were doing great missionary work and allowing the people group to dictate the gospel for themselves, when you arrived at church and you felt a bit culturally uncomfortable, then and only then was contextualization of the Gospel happening; but such contextualization does not happen when church looks the same way it does in your context. In other words, what do ministry leaders fear by allowing the Holy Spirit to move and contextualize worship, praise, and theology for the people and by the people?

25. Samuel Perry has found that the majority of Evangelical Outreach Ministries (EOMs) are managed and headed by Whites, making for a shift in the power dynamics in that community and organization. See Samuel L. Perry, "Racial Habitus, Moral Conflict, and White Moral Hegemony within Interracial Evangelical Organizations," *Qualitative Sociology* 35, no. 1 (2012): 93, 94. What might this, then, suggest about the views of future multi-ethnics on God, the Bible, and even life?

26. Perry continues that these types of EOMs do not structure much around racial awareness or identity, making this problematic, to say the least, in that ethnic minority youth are sterilized, in a manner, toward race and ethnicity; not very helpful when the issues of Ferguson and Michael Brown make their way to the EOM's doorstep. Perry, "Racial Habitus," 101-3.

27. James H. Cone, *God of the Oppressed* (New York: Seabury, 1975), 99-105; James H. Cone, *Black Theology and Black Power*, 5th ed. (Maryknoll, NY: Orbis, 1997).

28. I use rap and hip hop here because of its relevance to youth ministry and the rising tide of White/Euro-American suburban youth who admire rapper and hip hopper Tupac Amaru Shakur. In my own work I found that a large group of White/Euro-American youth identified with Tupac's lyrical message about God, pain, life, death, and Jesus. As a youth worker, this cannot be ignored. See Hodge, *Heaven has a Ghetto*.

29. For a broader view of this concept, see Tyron L. Inbody, *The Many Faces of Christology* (Nashville: Abingdon, 2002). For a discussion about the varieties of Jesus and Christology, see Volker Küster, *The Many Faces of Jesus Christ: Intercultural Christology* (Maryknoll, NY: Orbis, 2001).

30. To add, Native American and First Nations people groups are unresourced too. There is little to no material that deals with this group of young people and even less research that combines Christian theology, youth ministry, and culture into a practical guide and resource.

31. Rah, *The Next Evangelicalism*, 200.

32. As a director for a youth ministry centre, I get hundreds of calls dealing with a variety of youth ministry issues. One of the calls I am getting more of is that of incarcerated ethnic minority teens being released into suburban settings and youth pastors failing miserably in their approach to serve. Cases of segregation and even creating locked youth rooms have surfaced and these too need addressing.

33. Must reads are Cone, *God of the Oppressed*; Cone, *Black Theology and Black Power*; James Cone, *A Black Theology of Liberation*, 40th anniversary ed. (Maryknoll, NY: Orbis, 2010).

34. Choan-Seng Song, *Third-Eye Theology: Theology in Formation in Asian Settings* (Maryknoll, NY: Orbis, 1979).

35. Gustavo Gutiérrez, *On Job: God-Talk and the Suffering of the Innocent*, Trans. by Matthew J. O'Connell (Maryknoll, NY: Orbis, 1987).

36. Yancy, "Introduction," 6-10.

37. Daniel White Hodge, "Baptized in Dirty Water: An Ontology of Hip Hop's Manufacturing of Socio-Religious Discourse in Tupac's 'Black Jesuz,'" *Memphis Theological Seminary Journal* 50, no. 11 (2012): 201-202.

38. Ebony A. Utley, *Rap and Religion: Understanding the Gangsta's God* (Santa Barbara, CA: Praeger, 2012), 49.

39. Tom Beaudoin, *Virtual Faith: The Irreverent Spiritual Quest of Generation X* (San Francisco: Jossey-Bass, 1998), 123.

40. For more on this particular subject, see Don Cupitt, "Post-Christianity," in *Religion, Modernity, and Postmodernity*, ed. Paul Heelas, 218-32 (Oxford: Blackwell, 1998).

41. Hodge, "No Church in the Wild," 8.

42. Cone, *God of the Oppressed*, 161.

PART II

WISDOM

5.

Thriving Families

LISA SCANDRETTE AND MARK SCANDRETTE

Mark Scandrette is the founding director of ReIMAGINE: A Center for Integral Christian Practice. His books include *FREE* and *Soul Graffiti*. He frequently speaks on creative, radical, and embodied Christian practice.
Lisa Scandrette has devoted herself to a life of care, hospitality, and teaching children. She regularly facilitates workshops and provides administrative support for ReIMAGINE. In her spare time she loves creating with her hands.

Families today face many competing demands and challenges. Many are stretched by financial and time pressures, or by distractions and overwhelming choice. It can be hard to move together with purpose and stay connected. What's needed is an intentional approach to family life that is creative, soulful, and globally aware. Jesus offers a way of life that works. If our inherited ways of thinking, behaving, and relating are wearing us out and fragmenting our lives, Jesus offers a radical, integral alternative. What would our family lives look like if we let them be shaped more by this vision than by the values and priorities of a hurried and fragmented culture?

We believe that *a thriving family is a place of belonging and becoming, where each person feels safe, cared for, and loved, and is supported in order to develop who they are for the good of the world.* The trajectory of a thriving family is outward toward an ever-expanding embrace of the *shalom* that God desires for all people and all of creation. We seek to care for, connect, and belong to one another so we can be prepared to seek the greater good of all – so that all families on earth can thrive.

So much of our formation as people happens and is lived out in the context of family. That's where we develop our identity, where we learn what to value, how to relate to others, and how to navigate the challenges and stresses of life. Family is an important context of formation, not only for children, but for parents as well. We are all in the process of becoming who we were made to be for the good of the world.

Those of us who work with children, youth, and families long to see families thrive. We can take steps to strengthen our own family relationships, and we can encourage, support, and guide other families toward creating a thriving family culture. In this chapter, we will look at seven characteristics of thriving family culture and consider how families might take practical next steps in each area. You may want to work through these steps with your household and then invite other families in your faith community to join you in this process.

Carrying Out a Purpose

Your family can live from a deep sense of purpose and a positive vision of the future that you can articulate and use as a guide for decision-making.

When we were first married, we would often go for walks around Minnesota lakes and dream about the kind of family we wanted to be together. We wanted our home to be full of laughter and deep connection. We wanted our lives to be shaped by our awareness of God's purpose and presence. We wanted to do meaningful work together, using our gifts to serve. Early on, we felt we were getting traction and moving toward this dream. And then we had three kids in three years.

Suddenly, life was much more complicated. There were babies to feed, sleepless nights, diaper changes, so many physical needs. The financial and time pressures stretched us thin. On the surface, things looked good and stable. But our family life felt fragmented. While earlier we had felt competent in our skills for relating, we became aware of the gap that existed between the family that we dreamed of being and the one that we actually were.

One of the best things we did at that time was to stop and ask ourselves if the way we were living was working for us. Where were our choices leading us? Did we like where we were going? What were our choices teaching our children? We took time to explore new possibilities. We read books about creating healthy family culture and paid careful attention to the habits and rhythms of families we knew that seemed to be thriving. Inspired by what we read and saw, we decided to take some new steps.

One night, after the kids were in bed (they were too small to discuss family purpose with us at the time), we met to create a formal family purpose agreement. We spent some time praying and then brainstormed a two-page list of values and potential goals based on questions such as "What matters most to us?" and "What do we want to be about together?" Then we tried to distill our brainstorm into a few essential statements that looked something like this:

As a family we strive to
- *know and love God*
- *nurture healthy family relationships*
- *offer hospitality and care, especially to those who struggle and suffer*
- *use our gifts to serve*
- *live gratefully, creatively, and sustainably*

It was energizing to articulate and affirm what mattered most to us. We were so excited by this newfound clarity that we created a poster of our agreement and hung copies of it in the kitchen, on the bathroom mirror, and on the front door of our house. For the next few weeks, we read it aloud together every night at dinner. As we began using it to orient our family meetings, it became a compass that would guide us over the coming years.

Creating a family purpose agreement can be a powerful way to make your intentions explicit. Common agreements can help you make decisions about how you spend your time based what matters most to you. A shared purpose agreement can also help you move together in greater unity and solidarity by reminding you why you are choosing your daily activities and priorities.

Your family will benefit from articulating what you want to be about. Adult family members may want to begin shaping the family purpose agreement and then invite children to participate in the conversation. When you include the whole family in this process, each member feels greater ownership of the values, goals, and priorities that the family chooses. Below are some questions that may help guide your brainstorming:

- **The larger story.** *What do our faith, beliefs, and experiences tell us about what is of ultimate importance? Why are we here? What makes life meaningful? What is the purpose of human existence? Is there a passage of scripture that speaks to us about these questions – for example, a passage about loving God and neighbour, seeking God's kingdom, or doing justice, loving mercy, and walking humbly?*
- **Relationships.** *How do we want to care for and nurture one another? Who else are we committed to travelling with through the seasons of life (grandparents, aunts and uncles, cousins, friends, our faith community, our neighbourhood)?*
- **Vocation.** *How do we want to be of use in the world? What is our unique work, contribution, or calling as a family?*
- **Passions.** *Out of all that we could care about, what are we especially passionate about? How is each of us uniquely wired to seek the greater good?*
- **Values.** *What are the principles and ideals that we want to guide us?*

Melissa and her ex-husband, Michael, co-parent two high-needs children who are on the autism spectrum. "Because of our challenges," Melissa says, "our family purpose agreement is focused on boundaries and basics: Pray. Be kind. Show respect. Be grateful. Love God and people. Work on yourself so you have something to give."

After you've had the opportunity to dream together, distill your family's purpose into five to seven succinct words or phrases. Post your purpose statement somewhere your family can see it and be reminded of it.

Finding a Rhythm

Families can enact household rhythms and policies that are life-giving and that support the family's shared purpose. Rhythms are regular and repeated pockets of time spent on specific activities. If we value something, we need to make time to live it out along with the other daily details. It needs to show up on our calendar. Most of us already have some rhythms in our lives, such as bedtime routines, family meals, or routines that help us get out the door in the morning. We can make intentional choices to establish new rhythms that help us create spaces in which to live out our deeper purpose. When we embed our values in a rhythm, these values become easier to live out because we don't have to think about them every time; they become part of the fabric of our lives.

When our kids were small, one of Lisa's favourite family rhythms was something we called "Dad and Kid Night," which was really just code for "Mom's Night Out." At the time, Lisa was home all day with three small children. She needed time to recharge and have some space to herself. Mark needed to connect with the kids after working all day. So on Dad and Kid Night, Mark would come home promptly and Lisa would leave as soon as he did. Mark would feed the kids dinner, do something fun with them, and put them to bed. Meanwhile, Lisa would go out. She might meet a friend, wander around a bookstore, even get groceries unhindered, and she often returned after everyone else in the house was sleeping. It was great for her. But it was also something the kids really counted on. When the time for Dad and Kid Night came around, if Lisa was slow to get out the door one of the kids would inevitably ask, "Mom, aren't you going to leave? It's Dad and Kid Night! You should be going." It was a winning rhythm for all of us for many years.

You can connect the activities of your life to your deeper purpose. Ask the following questions and discuss them together as a family:

- *What rhythms will help us live into our family purpose?*
- *When and how during the week will we connect as partners, as a family, and as parent and child?*
- *What are the daily, weekly, and yearly rhythms we would like to pursue and enact?*

Choose at least one new rhythm to enact that will help you live into your family's purpose.

Sharing a Common Story

Families can cultivate awakening to God's care and the larger story we are all part of by embracing life-giving spiritual practices and making conscious ethical choices. Many parents wonder if they're qualified to guide their child's understanding of God's story. We might feel pressure to impress exactly the right beliefs or practices on our kids, or hesitate to share much of anything because we don't want to say the wrong thing. Isn't this a job best left to the professionals? But as children's and youth ministry leaders, we know that parents have a much greater impact on faith formation than any weekly program can offer.

Families have the tremendous opportunity to explore the most important questions of human existence together. Why is this such an important task for families? Because we live up to the stories we live under. Your understanding of the true story of the world significantly shapes how you belong to one another and who you are becoming together. To say it another way: this is the *why* behind your family purpose agreement. As a family, you can learn to explore the basic questions of human existence – God's story – in ways that are honest, truthful, compassionate, and hopeful. You don't need to have all the answers before you invite one another on this journey. The important thing is learning to engage these questions together to discover how to live a beautiful story.

Many families benefit from taking regular time together to acknowledge God's presence and reflect on the larger story. Whatever stage the people in your family are at, there are ways to explore the larger story together. You could read and discuss scriptures together, or read a book or watch a movie and have a conversation about the themes and how they connect with God's larger story and the human condition. You could tell the story of your own faith journey – the experiences that shaped you, how your understanding has changed over time, what you believe, and why. Pray together as a way to remember the Creator's presence and care. It's not necessary to have all the "right" answers. We're on this story-exploring journey together. Stay curious and lean into questions while also sharing what you believe to be true.

The following questions might be good prompts for beginning to discuss what your family is discovering to be true about the real story of the world:

- *What kind of world do we live in? Where did this world come from and who is in charge? What is God like?*
- *Who are we as human beings? What kind of creatures are we?*
- *Why are we here? What are people for? What is our quest?*
- *What is the basic struggle of humanity? What threatens human flourishing?*
- *What is the path to awakening, enlightenment, salvation and eternal life? How can we recover the good lives we were created for?*

Fostering Connection

It's important for family members to relate to one another with love and respect, and to pursue healthy ways to connect, communicate, navigate conflicts, and have fun. We need to belong before we can become. A warm, positive home is both a gift of grace and the result of an intentional practice.

One of our family's favourite ways to create this kind of space is to occasionally "do a round of affirmations" at the dinner table. We tend to do this whenever we feel the people in our family could use a little extra care. We go around the table and take turns saying specific things we appreciate about each person, such as, "You really know how to make me laugh," "You have lots of curiosity and passion for learning," or "You are really persistent when something is hard for you." At first it might be hard for some family members to express affirmation or receive praise. But our words can be a powerful way to show love to each other and, like most things, we get better at it with practice.

How should we treat each other? Chances are that if you ask that of the members of your family, even the youngest ones will be able to articulate what love and respect look like. They might respond with things like "speak kindly," "tell the truth," "listen," "respect other people's things," "respect other people's bodies," or "don't hit." Your family can establish agreed-upon ground rules for living together that can help each member relate in ways that build your family's connection.

However, we don't always treat each other with the love and respect we each deserve. We get angry. We say hurtful words. We fail to communicate. We don't follow through on our commitments. When family ground rules are broken, it can cause ruptures in relationships. When this happens, families can take steps to make repairs by admitting mistakes, seeking forgiveness, and building greater understanding. In fact, making repairs strengthens relationships. Many families find it helpful to have an established process for working through conflict. Here are some helpful steps:

- **Stop and talk.** *What are the ground rules you both agree to follow when you're working through conflict?*
- **Listen to each other.** *What happened, or what's not working? How does this make you feel?*
- **Own your part.** *What part of this conflict can you own? What would you like the other person to acknowledge?*
- **Give and receive forgiveness.** *What do you need to ask forgiveness for? What are you ready to forgive?*
- **Affirm love.** *What can you say right now to affirm your love and commitment to each other?*

- **Explore solutions.** *What can be done to correct the situation? Is this an opportunity to clarify better expectations or negotiate a new household policy?*

It can be particularly powerful when a parent can admit to a child that they were wrong and ask for forgiveness. In our family we've often needed to apologize to our kids, saying something like, "It's important for me to guide and correct you, but how I just spoke to you was wrong. It came from anger and impatience. Will you forgive me?" When you apologize to your kids, you show real strength and create a space of healing and reconciliation that they can trust and emulate.

It's also crucial that parents come alongside their kids to help them learn to manage ruptures that occur with their siblings, friends, or themselves. Sibling relationships contribute significantly to family culture. At their best, brothers and sisters provide support and encouragement to one another as lifelong allies. Still, conflicts between siblings are common and, when left unresolved, can threaten the health of their relationship and their family culture of love and respect. Teaching children to navigate conflict takes work. It may be tempting to silence the squabbling, judge the situation, or prescribe a solution. But if you take the time to facilitate and teach conflict resolution skills, you'll be equipping them for a lifetime of peacemaking in all of their relationships.

Nurturing Growth

At their best, our families gently hold our brokenness, affirm our belovedness, and support our becoming. One of the tricky things about family life is that our family members see us at both our best and our worst. When we are out in public, we can carefully manage the parts of us that others see, but our families see us when we are tired, sick, stressed, or struggling. And in those times, we often find that we have developed ways of coping that are less than whole. We need to find ways to co-operate with God's remaking in our lives.

One of our goals as a family is to effectively grow toward our best selves – in other words, become like Christ in our character and behavior

– by celebrating our blessedness and being honest about our broken-ness. We believe it's important for us, as adult family members, to model authenticity and vulnerability. We all have gaps between how we want to live and how we actually live. Character growth is a lifelong process, not a one-time event or something only children need. Modelling honesty and vulnerability shows our kids that we don't expect anything of them that we do not expect of ourselves. And as we learn and grow, we can also provide them with a model for their own paths toward growth.

One way that our family has found it helpful to address the places where we feel the invitation to grow and change is by developing what we call an "experiment in truth." An experiment helps us to choose practices that might make a difference in the way we live our lives. For example, in recent years Lisa has struggled with feeling anxious. God's desire for us is to be at peace, because we are loved and cared for. When Lisa is anxious, it's because she believes that she has to be in control of the circumstances of life in order for things to be well. But she is not in control of everything. However, she is promised that nothing can separate her from what is essential, and she's invited to remember that in the Creator's presence she is safe.

Simply knowing this doesn't always change the anxiety she feels, so mind and body practices help her live in this reality. For a time, Lisa worried about our kids, as they had recently started college. She allowed herself to think and worry about them all day long. She decided that she'd meditatively knit gifts for them as a practice for managing anxiety. Each day, she devoted about ten minutes to knitting for each of them. As she knit, Lisa prayed about her concerns for each of them and reminded herself that God cares about them even more than we do. When she finished knitting for the day, it was her cue that she also needed to set down the concerns of their lives for the day.

She's also found that getting some physical exercise lessens her anxiety and worry. At other times, it has been helpful to memorize a passage of scripture, such as, "I will lie down and sleep in peace, for you alone, O LORD, make me dwell in safety" (Ps 4:8). Since she committed to these practices, over time her anxiety has decreased and she has come to experience more peace.

Take some time to develop your own "experiment in truth" by identifying one area where you want to respond to the invitation to grow and change. Work through the steps below to develop a plan you are ready to commit to.

- *What's not working? Where do you feel stuck? How would you like to experience growth and change in your life (such as finding better ways to manage stress or navigating life without worry and fear)?*
- *What are the patterns of choices that support your current behaviour?*
- *What are the underlying scripts or thought patterns that drive your current behaviour patterns (such as jealousy, resentment, insecurity, fear, anger)?*
- *Imagine the life that is possible. What is reality? What is the good vision of life God makes possible that you are being invited into (for example, I am God's beloved child. I have everything I need to thrive in this moment. Perfect love casts away all fear.)*
- *How do you want to respond? What mind, body, and relational limits and practices can help you cooperate with the Spirit's work in your life?*

Our growth edges are the places where we have the opportunity to experience more of God's grace and wholeness in our lives. To experience growth and change, it helps to have the support of the people closest to us. It takes patience and grace to become more whole as humans. In family, we can frame the need for growth in a positive light and make it a normal part of the culture. We can cheer each other on along the way, and celebrate that growth when we see it.

Celebrating Abundance

We are all in search of the right-sized life, one with just the right amount of time, money, and possessions. We live in a culture that has lost its sense of proportion, in which the answer to "what's the right-sized life?" always seems to be "more, bigger, and better." Our oversized lives make us stressed, sick, and tired, and strain the earth's resources. While we struggle to keep things right-sized, many of our global brothers and sisters struggle to have enough. Knowing that we live in a world of great inequity and ecological decline, we're also invited to ask what the right-sized life is so that every family on the planet can thrive. A thriving family lives abundantly, uses its resources wisely, and practices gratitude, contentment, trust, and generosity.

Perhaps a first step in celebrating abundance is practicing gratitude. Gratitude helps us to reframe how we see our lives and invites us to recognize and enjoy how we are already provided for. With practice, your family can cultivate gratitude together. You may want to start, perhaps each evening around the dinner table, by inviting each person in your family to share one thing they are grateful for from their day. Naturally you might include big items like family or health, but also try to mention small things that bring you delight, like hearing a favourite song, popcorn, your dog's playful companionship, or the turning of autumn leaves. Be as specific as you can. Gratitude helps us see the abundance that we have in our lives.

In a right-sized life, our possessions enhance our goals in some way; they have a practical purpose or they bring beauty into our lives. When we have too many things, it can be hard to enjoy them all, and they take time and effort to maintain. Curating and editing your possessions can help you spend your time and energy on what matters most.

Similarly, we can also free ourselves to celebrate abundance by finding a right-sized way to deal with our finances. Creating a spending plan can help you determine where you need to spend your resources and thus align your spending with your family goals. Can you make room for all that matters to your family in your spending plan? If not, you can explore possible trade-offs. Perhaps you will need to spend less in one area so that you can spend more in an area that matters more to you. You may also find it helpful to have a spending plan for your time as well as you finances.

Living a right-sized life helps us to use our resources in life-giving ways for ourselves and for others. We live in a world of abundance, and those of us who live among the wealthiest in the world have the opportunity to share that abundance with those who are struggling to have enough. We can choose to limit ourselves by adopting more sustainable and ethical practices so that we can share with those who have less. What next step can your family take to support another family who struggles, or to live more sustainably on the earth?

Supporting Productivity

Your family can celebrate and support each person's uniqueness and their development of skills and capacities that serve others and pursue the greater good.

There are two kinds of work to do in a family. First, there is the work we do to take care of the business of life: acquiring and preparing food, cleaning and maintaining our space, managing finances, attending doctor appointments, and seeing to all the other physical needs of our family. Taking care of this work can be a great way for families to share life and connect. We can transfer these skills from the older people in our family to the younger ones as we first work together and then hand over the work to the children as they gain the ability to do it themselves. Thus we build capacity and confidence as we each contribute to the life of the family in age-appropriate ways.

Second, there is the work that each person is uniquely gifted to do for the good of the world. As a family, we have the opportunity to become students of one another, learning to affirm each other's gifts, encourage passions, and provide each other with opportunities and resources that help us discover what we were made to do.

Our middle child's first word was "actually," which was a good clue as to how he saw the world. Noah has always been interested in knowing and explaining how things work. When he was twelve, he began chronicling the area's birds, eventually documenting over 120 species. He kept bird songs on his iPod and recognized many birds by their call. He loved explaining what he was learning, but hadn't yet figured out how to share his knowledge in the most gracious ways. So when a teacher asked him to help teach younger children in a nature class, we felt it was a perfect opportunity for him to learn to share what he knew and to be mentored by someone who shared his interests. Later, he became an "explainer" at a local hands-on science museum. That experience exposed him to working scientists and gave him a chance to teach the public. He's now pursuing a degree in physics, while also tutoring and working in a research lab. We often talk about what he might do with his set of skills for the good of the world. Perhaps he will create a more efficient fuel cell, or develop technology that will help supply water in the developing world.

As a family, we can support each other in discovering where our giftings and the *shalom* the Creator desires for our world intersect. While we do this we can also include others in that sense of belonging that we've cultivated. Pay attention to the struggles in your immediate surroundings. What aches do you see among your family, friends, and neighbours? Learn about global issues and imagine together how you can make connections between different struggles and the interests or abilities you have. Then look for places to have first-hand experiences with the aches and struggles of our world. We tend to be around people most like ourselves, so we might need to be intentional about crossing boundaries so that we can connect with the beauty and challenges of other communities. Perhaps your family could take public transportation, shop at a different grocery store, or find a place where you can connect regularly with an at-risk community, such as a nursing home or homeless shelter. Look for practical and creative ways to serve and love the people around you. Invite someone who is lonely or far from home to spend time with your family. Bring a meal to someone who is sick or having a difficult time. Let your kids lead the way with their ideas of how to bring love to people.

Three Essential Tools

As you continue along this road to belonging, becoming, and creating a thriving family culture, we'd like to suggest three tools that will be helpful.

First, take some time for reflection. We invite you to slow down and think about the dreams you have for your family, what you'd like to bring into your family from your past, and what you would like to leave behind. As we cultivate self-awareness, we are more likely to make conscious decisions about our actions.

Second, find a time to meet as the adults of the household. It takes time, work, and intentionality to live into your family's purpose. Use this time to check in on your schedules, reach common agreements, and make plans for any new steps you'd like to take toward family thriving. You may want to follow this up with a whole-family meeting that involves the younger members of your family in the decision-making process.

Finally, make time for whole-household activities. Families benefit from having set aside times to talk, listen, learn, laugh, and take action together.

The journey toward family thriving is about process, not perfection. Resist the urge to compare your family to others. Your family has a unique gift for the world. Embrace your power and remember that all family members – old or young, tall or small – shape family culture. You can say yes to God's good desires for the life of your family. Together we can create a thriving culture for our families, our communities, and our world.

Make our families places of belonging and becoming:
one in purpose,
together in rhythm,
united by a common story.
Help us connect with love and respect,
growing in wisdom,
living abundantly
and productively seeking the greater good,
so that our families and every family on earth can thrive.

This chapter is adapted by Mark and Lisa Scandrette from their book *Belonging and Becoming: Creating a Thriving Family Culture*, published by InterVarsity Press, 2016. *Belonging and Becoming* includes a group learning guide and plenty of discussion questions and exercises to help families thrive.

6.

Conceptions of and Commitments to Children

Biblical Wisdom for Families, Congregations, and the Worldwide Church

MARCIA J. BUNGE

Marcia J. Bunge, Ph.D., is Professor of Religion and the Bernhardson Distinguished Chair of Lutheran Studies at Gustavus Adolphus College in Saint Peter, Minnesota. She has edited and contributed to four volumes on religious views of children, including *The Child in the Bible* and *The Child in Christian Thought*.

Just a few miles south of Chicago's St. James Episcopal Cathedral (where Faith Forward gatherings have been held since 2015) is the University of Chicago. I went to graduate school there to study historical theology. Even though this university is world-renowned, and even though I later pursued research in some of the best universities in Germany, throughout graduate school I did not have to study anything about children. At that time, the subject of children was seen as marginal in the field of theology. It was considered to be "beneath" the serious theologian and primarily meant for people who liked working with children, such as Sunday school teachers, religious educators, or youth pastors.

However, two big experiences turned my attention to children: becoming the mother of two, and teaching undergraduates. Having children at home and being surrounded by 18- to 22-year-olds at work led me to start asking a lot of questions about what was going on with children and youth in our schools, churches, and society. As a scholar, I also started to wonder: did any Christian theologians or ethicists address the needs of children? Why isn't childhood a burning topic for the whole church, especially when children are in our congregations, and when one-third of all people on the planet are children? These and other questions radically changed the focus of my research to children and childhood.

I quickly discovered that childhood is not a marginal topic in the Bible, in Christian theology, or in other world religions, and over the past few years I have published four volumes on religious understandings of children and childhood.[1] Furthermore, the field of childhood studies is now a growing area of intellectual inquiry in many disciplines; not only education and psychology, but also theology, religious studies, law, sociology, literature, history, and philosophy.

Two important questions that are raised in my research and the growing interdisciplinary field of childhood studies and that are important for all of us in the church today are:

1. What are our conceptions of children? How do we think about and perceive children in our families, communities, or culture? What are they? Who are they?
2. What are our *commitments to them*? What are our obligations? Our responsibilities? What do we owe children?

Conceptions of and commitments to children vary over time and across cultures; they are also closely interrelated. On the one hand, if we hold a narrow and simplistic conception of children, then our commitments to them are bound to be thin and one-dimensional. On the other hand, if we have a complex and multifaceted view of children, then it is likely that our obligations and relationships to them will also be robust and multi-dimensional.

One of the most fruitful ways for those of us in the church to reflect on these two central questions, and thereby broaden our perspectives, is to take a fresh look at the church's most authoritative text: the Bible. My chapter aims to reflect on these two questions by exploring six biblical *conceptions* of and *commitments* to children, and by emphasizing the need to *incorporate all six perspectives* in our interactions with children.[2] My primary thesis is that *although Christians today and in the past have often viewed children in narrow and even destructive ways, the Bible expresses six insightful and central perspectives on children and our obligations to them. By holding these six perspectives in tension (rather than in isolation), we can broaden our conceptions of children and strengthen our commitments to them within families and all areas of the church.*

By going back to the Bible and understanding and appreciating biblical conceptions of and commitments to children, I hope that all of us can discover ways to renew and strengthen our own conceptions of and commitments to the children in our midst and those around the world. I have included some questions to reflect on as we journey through these perspectives.

Six Biblical Perspectives on Conceptions of and Obligations to Children

1.
CONCEPTION: CHILDREN ARE GIFTS OF GOD AND SOURCES OF JOY.
COMMITMENT: ENJOY AND BE GRATEFUL FOR THEM!

The Bible and our rich Christian tradition often depict children as gifts of God and sources of joy who ultimately come from God and belong to God. Since they are gifts of God and sources of joy, adults are to enjoy children and be grateful for them. Many passages in the Bible speak of children as gifts of God, signs of God's blessing, or sources of joy. In Genesis, Sarah rejoices at the birth of her son, Isaac (Gen 21:6-7). In Luke, the angel promises Zechariah and Elizabeth that their child will bring them "joy and gladness" (Lk 1:14). In the gospel of John, Jesus says, "When a woman is in labour, she has pain...but when her child is born, she no longer remembers the anguish because of the joy of having brought a human being into the world" (Jn 16:21).[3]

Many Christian theologians have emphasized this biblical theme. For example, the 17th century Moravian bishop, theologian, and educator Comenius states that children are dearer than "gold and silver, than pearls and gems."[4] Martin Luther, the 16th century reformer who was the biological father of three sons and three daughters and took in four orphans, says children are "treasures from heaven," "blessings from God," and "great gifts."

REFLECTION

When have you experienced joy or delight around or with children or youth? What examples come to your mind?

2.
CONCEPTION: CHILDREN ARE FULLY HUMAN AND MADE IN THE IMAGE OF GOD.
COMMITMENT: TREAT THEM WITH DIGNITY AND RESPECT!

The Bible and the Christian tradition also emphasize that children are whole and complete human beings who are made in the image of God. They are fully human. Thus, adults are to treat children with dignity and respect. The basis of this claim is Genesis 1:27, which states that God made humankind, male and female, in God's image. It follows that children, like adults, possess the fullness of humanity. Regardless of race, gender, age, or class, they have intrinsic value.

Although most of us might think it is self-evident that infants and children are human beings, in many places and times, including here and now, children have not been considered fully human. Over the centuries they have been described and perceived as: "property," "animals," "beasts," "pre-rational," "pre-human," "almost human," "not quite human," or "on their way to being human." Roman law, for example, considered children to be property, and a father could legally allow unwanted infants to die. But contrary to Roman law, early

Christians, like Jews, consistently rejected infanticide. Early theologians, such as Cyprian, said all people, even infants, are "alike and equal since they have been made once by God." All share a "divine and spiritual equality."[5]

All of us know too well that children are treated as less than human in many ways (whether in homes, churches, or schools; whether within our own country or in other countries around the world). At the same time, we also know that the simple act of truly affirming the full humanity of children can have life-changing and inspiring results!

One man who has inspired me (and thousands of others) to view all children as fully human is Shiferaw Woldemichael. He was once a human rights lawyer and even the Attorney General of Ethiopia. But he realized that his country could not flourish if it did not support children. So he gave up his law practice and started divisions of Compassion International in Ethiopia and Tanzania. He then founded and directed the Child Development Training and Research Centre, which is one of the most significant child-focused centres in Africa. He has a heart for children and sees each one as fully human, even the most marginal of the marginal: children in poverty, sexually-exploited girls, or AIDS/HIV orphans.

REFLECTION
Who or what inspires us to see all children as fully human?

3.
CONCEPTION: CHILDREN ARE VULNERABLE
ORPHANS, NEIGHBOURS, AND STRANGERS.
COMMITMENT: PROVIDE FOR, PROTECT, AND
SEEK JUSTICE FOR CHILDREN (NOT JUST YOUR
OWN CHILDREN BUT ALL CHILDREN IN NEED)!
Many biblical passages emphasize, in the third place,
that children are also orphans, neighbours, and strangers; they are voiceless and among the most vulnerable people on the planet, and as such are often victims of injustice. The Bible also commands adults to provide

for, protect, and seek justice for all children, including orphans, the poor, and the marginalized. Adults are to care not only for their own children but also for all children in need. Numerous biblical passages explicitly command us to love and to seek justice for the most vulnerable: widows, orphans, and strangers. Deuteronomy 10:18, for example, states that God is a God "who executes justice for the orphan and the widow, and who loves the strangers, providing them food and clothing."

Christian obligations to children in need are also grounded in Jesus' command to "love the Lord your God with all your heart" and to "love your neighbour [and even your enemies] as yourself" (Mk 10:31). In the gospels, Jesus shows compassion directly to children. He welcomes them, receives them, touches them, and heals them. He takes them up in his arms and blesses them.

Informed by these and other passages, Christians in the past and Christians around the world today help feed and clothe poor children and orphans. They value adoption and support those who adopt, and are outspoken advocates for children's rights and political policies that protect children and families. This commitment to children in need is a task shared among Christian families, congregations, and a host of national and international faith-based organizations (agencies, hospitals, clinics, orphanages, and child advocacy and lobbying ministries). There are many powerful stories of Christians who looked outside their doorways, saw children in need, and responded. In many cases, their efforts blossomed into thriving institutions. I am sure that each of us can find examples of people in our own faith community who have shown compassion to children.

Two people from my own Lutheran tradition are A. H. Franke (1663-1727) and Leymah Gbowee (born 1972). Francke was a 17th century pastor who saw tremendous suffering and poverty in his town of Halle, Germany. In response, he opened an orphanage in his home. He began with three or four children and no funding, but within a few years he had established a vast and famous set of institutions called the *Franckesche Stiftungen*. These included an orphanage, a pharmacy, a publishing house, schools for rich and poor alike, and the first German pediatric hospital.

Leymah Gbowee is a Lutheran woman who won the Nobel Peace Prize in 2011 for helping to end the terrible 14-year civil war in Liberia. During the war she witnessed girls being raped and boys being taken as child soldiers. Starting with just a prayer group in her church, she was able to gather together hundreds of Christian and Muslim women to form a non-violent peace movement that helped end that dreadful civil war.

REFLECTION

What stories of compassion for children do you tell in your family or church? What institutions or initiatives do you admire? Consider telling these stories of authentic service especially to children and youth in your midst. They might not know how adults in the church are caring for others, and such stories are powerful.

4.

CONCEPTION: CHILDREN ARE DEVELOPING BEINGS WHO NEED INSTRUCTION AND GUIDANCE.

COMMITMENT: INSTRUCT, GUIDE, AND BRING THEM UP IN THE FAITH, HELPING THEM TO LOVE GOD AND THE NEIGHBOUR!

A fourth central perspective of children that is expressed in the Bible and in Christian traditions is that children are developing beings who need instruction and guidance. Adults are to bring up children in the faith, helping them to love God and their neighbours as themselves.

Several biblical texts address these responsibilities. For example, Christians, like Jews, refer to the famous lines from Deuteronomy 6:5-7: "You shall love the Lord your God with all your heart, and with all your soul, and with all your might. Keep these words that I am commanding you today in your heart. Recite them to your children and talk about them when you are at home and when you are away, when you lie down and when you rise." This and other texts encourage us to be teaching and talking about faith with children and youth at all times.

There are also many examples in Christian tradition of theologians who took seriously the spiritual formation and education of children. For example, John Chrysostom in the fourth century,[6] Martin Luther and John Calvin in the 16th century, Comenius in the 17th century, and Schleiermacher in the 19th century all wrote and preached about faith formation for children. They also wrote catechisms and other materials for use in the home to help parents teach their children. In his *Large Catechism*, Luther said, "If we want able and qualified persons as civil and spiritual leaders, then we really must spare no toil, trouble, or cost in teaching and educating our children to serve God and humanity."[7]

These theologians, the Bible, and, indeed, common sense all tell us that faith formation is a cooperative and intergenerational task involving home, congregation, and the wider church. Faith formation is the task of neither parents alone nor the church alone. We cannot "out-source" or "in-source" this task. We have to do it together. Parents, church leaders, and other caring adults help to nurture the moral and spiritual lives of children in a number of ways and through a variety of spiritual practices, such as reading the Bible, worshipping, praying, singing, serving others, or participating in the sacraments. All of these practices have a very long tradition in the church throughout the world. They are powerful vehicles that can create space for the Holy Spirit to work in our lives, and open our hearts (at any age) to God and the neighbour. Christian communities also incorporate such practices into a host of creative programs, initiatives, and activities for young people, such as: youth and family ministries, religious education programs, Bible camps, music camps, national youth conventions, campus ministries, service projects, and mission trips. This book you are reading is, in fact, filled with creative ideas for nurturing children and youth.

REFLECTION
Which practices helped deepen your own faith as you grew up? Which ones are helping to deepen the faith of children in your midst?

5.

CONCEPTION: CHILDREN ARE SINFUL CREATURES AND SOCIAL AGENTS WITH GROWING MORAL CAPACITIES AND RESPONSIBILITIES.

COMMITMENT: MODEL FOR THEM COMPASSION AND ACCOUNTABILITY, AND CULTIVATE WITH THEM PRACTICES OF MUTUAL CONFESSION, FORGIVENESS, AND RENEWAL!

Many, but certainly not all, forms of Christianity express the notion that children are not just developing beings; they are also, in some sense, sinful creatures and moral agents with growing moral capacities and responsibilities. Adults can help children by modelling compassion and accountability, and cultivating practices and patterns of confession, forgiveness, and renewal with them.

The view of children as sinful is based on the interpretations of several biblical texts. For example, Genesis states that every inclination of the human heart is "evil from youth" (Gen 8:21), and Proverbs claim that folly is "bound up in the heart" of children (Prov 22:15). The Psalms declare that "the wicked go astray from the womb; they err from their birth" (Ps 58:3; cf. 51:5). Paul writes that all people are "under the power of sin," and "there is no one who is righteous, not even one" (Rom 3: 9-10; cf. 5:12).

Christian theologians who view children as sinful generally underscore two related points. On the one hand, they often claim children are "born in a state of sin"; they live in a world that is not what it ought to be. Their parents are not perfectly loving and just; social institutions that support them, such as schools and governments, are not free from corruption; and the communities in which they live, no matter how safe, are not free of injustice and violence. On the other hand, theologians who speak of children as sinful also claim that children possess growing moral capacities and responsibilities and that, as they develop, they sometimes carry out "actual sins." They can sometimes act in ways that are self-centred, unjust, and harmful to themselves and others; they sometimes miss the mark, and hurt others. Thus, they bear some degree of responsibility for their actions.

On the surface, viewing children as sinful can seem negative and destructive. And as some historical studies have shown, viewing children exclusively as sinful has often warped Christian approaches to children and led in some cases to child abuse and even death. However, the notion that children are sinful corrects an equally simplistic and dangerous view of children as primarily pure and innocent. Such a view leaves no room for appreciating a child's own growing moral agency or levels of accountability; nor does it encourage talking to children about social and individual wrongdoing.

Thus, the language of children as sinful, when used cautiously and with attention to child development, can strengthen our awareness of a child's growing moral capacity and ability to assume responsibility. It lets us talk with children about human mistakes and shortcomings – theirs and ours – and the lifelong importance of forgiving ourselves and others. Since children experience both the sins of others and their own sins against others, and since adults are certainly also sinners, adults can help children by modelling compassion and accountability. Adults can also cultivate with children practices and patterns of confession, forgiveness, and renewal. Social scientists say that few parents say to their children, "I'm sorry." Yet when we say to children, "I'm sorry. I made a mistake. Can you forgive me?" we teach them much about us and about them and we create deep adult-child connections.

REFLECTION

As you think about your relationships with children, how have you helped them develop responsibility and the language for confession and forgiveness (of self and others)? How have you helped them learn practices of confessing sins and asking for forgiveness? What is your experience?

6.

CONCEPTION: CHILDREN ARE MODELS OF FAITH WHO ARE ENDOWED WITH PARTICULAR STRENGTHS, GIFTS, AND TALENTS IN ORDER THAT THEY MAY CONTRIBUTE TO THE COMMON GOOD NOW AND IN THE FUTURE.

COMMITMENT: LISTEN TO AND LEARN FROM THEM! HONOUR THEIR CONTRIBUTIONS! PROVIDE THEM WITH AN EDUCATION!

The Bible does not just speak about children as sinful and in need of instruction. Rather, the Bible also claims that children are often models of faith for adults, and that they are endowed with particular strengths, gifts, and talents in order that they may contribute to the common good now and in the future. Thus, adults do not just teach children. From a biblical perspective, we are to listen to and learn from them, honour their current relationship with God, respect their contributions to family and community, and provide them with an excellent education so that they can continue to cultivate their gifts and talents and contribute to the common good.

The Bible depicts children and young people as models of faith, agents of positive change, and prophets, and it does so in striking and even radical ways. Take, for example, the story of the boy Samuel (1 Sam 2-4) and the one of young David (1 Sam 17).

Further, in all three synoptic gospels Jesus identifies himself with children and lifts them up as paradigms of receiving the reign of God, saying, "Truly I tell you, whoever does not receive the kingdom of God as a little child will never enter it" (Mk 10:13-16). All three synoptic gospels also give an account of Jesus welcoming and blessing little children. (See Mk 10:13-16; cf. Lk 18:15-17; Mt 19:13-15; also Mt 18:2-5; Mk 9:33-37; Lk 9:46-48.)

The Bible also proclaims that children are Spirit-filled. God's Spirit is not limited by the age of any person; it is already working in children and young people. You cannot stop God's Spirit. Biblical passages depict children and infants praising God (Ps 8:2; Mt 21:15). As the book of Acts declares, God's Spirit will be poured out "upon all flesh, and your sons and your daughters shall prophesy, and your young men shall see visions" (Acts 2:17; cf. Jl 2:28-32).

In the above examples, the Bible depicts children variously as: Spirit-filled, models for adults, agents of positive change, prophets, and endowed with gifts and talents. Children are to listen to and obey adults, but their highest loyalty is to God. Indeed, most serious theologians who discuss parental authority claim that it is never absolute, because a child's ultimate loyalty is to God. And building on biblical texts, they claim that adults should not provoke children to anger (Col 3:21; Eph 6:4). As Luther said, "Parental authority is strictly limited; it does not extend to the point where it can wreak damage and destruction to the child, especially to its soul."[8]

REFLECTION
Can you add insights from your own experience about the strengths, gifts, and contributions of children?

Holding All Six Perspectives in Tension

A strong and biblically-based view of children holds all six perspectives in tension rather than isolation. Although all six perspectives provide us with a rich view of children and adult-child relationships, Christianity has often focused narrowly on only one or two of these biblical themes. However, if we neglect any of them our conceptions of children become narrow and distorted and we risk treating children in inadequate and harmful ways.

There are many examples of such neglect in the church. For example, if we say that children are primarily gifts of God and sources of joy, then we might delight in them but neglect to nurture and guide them. Or if we believe that children are primarily sinful and in need of instruction, then we might do much to educate them but neglect to delight in them and enjoy them. Or if we view children primarily as victims, we might not hear their voices and recognize their strengths and agency. Or if we perceive children mainly as social agents and participants, then we might recognize their gifts and strengths but neglect to protect and guide them. Certainly, too, if we focus primarily on nurturing only our "own" children, then we might overlook the responsibility of reaching out to all children in need.

We can avoid these and other dangers by incorporating a complex view of children that holds together these six biblical perspectives. We need to cultivate a child-inclusive and biblically-based perspective that views children, paradoxically, as

- *fully human and made in the image of God, yet also still developing and in need of instruction and guidance;*
- *gifts of God and sources of joy, yet also capable of selfish and sinful actions;*
- *vulnerable and in need of protection, yet also strong, insightful, and endowed with gifts to serve others and act as models of faith.*

The Bible urges us to wear multi-focal and inclusive lenses as we regard children – to switch from mono-focal tunnel vision to multi-focal perspectives – because stronger conceptions of children also strengthen our commitments to, and relationships with, them.

REFLECTION
What examples of narrow conceptions of children do you see in your context, whether it be your daily life, your congregation, or the broader culture? What dangers do you see? What are your experiences? How can these conceptions become more multi-focal?

Life-Giving Possibilities

If we as Christians can appropriate and hold in tension all six biblical perspectives of children, then we will certainly broaden our conceptions of children and strengthen our commitments to them, within the contexts of both family and church. For example, holding these six biblical perspectives of children in tension (rather than isolation) can help us do the following:

- *Strengthen child-adult relationships in all types of families;*
- *Enrich the church's worship life as well as its spiritual formation and religious education programs;*
- *Strengthen specific child, youth, family, and intergenerational ministries;*
- *Emphasize the importance of the family in spiritual formation and faith development;*
- *Advance the church's child advocacy efforts nationally and internationally;*
- *Strengthen theological education at seminaries and colleges around*
  the world so that they include attention to children.

Complex and biblically-informed theological understandings of children have many implications for our interactions with children within family, church, and neighbourhood, and for our child advocacy efforts in our own country and around the world. By critically appropriating a view of children that incorporates these six central perspectives, we can all take up more wholeheartedly and responsibly the Christian call to love and care for all children. We can do this from within our own setting, whether that be the area of spiritual formation, religious education, children's ministries, youth ministry, child protection and advocacy, faith-based organizations that work with young people who are at risk, or theological education.

When we are informed by a solid theological understanding of children, all of us can renew and strengthen our relationships with and commitments to the children in our midst and others around the world. Seeing through complex and multi-focal lenses allows us to work for and with children in our quests to build and enliven the church and contribute to the common good.

REFLECTION:

As you think of your own conceptions of and commitments to children

- *What biblical (or other) perspectives of children would you add to the list of six?*
- *How might biblical perspectives and obligations to children strengthen your commitments to the children in your midst and others around the world? What biblical passages open up a fresh perspective on your view of children and your commitments to them?*
- *What conception or intentional commitment is ready to blossom in your work and daily life today?*

1. See Marcia J. Bunge, ed., *Children, Adults, and Shared Responsibilities: Jewish, Christian, and Muslim Perspectives* (Cambridge: Cambridge University Press, 2012); Don Browning and Marcia J. Bunge, eds., *Children and Childhood in World Religions: Primary Sources and Texts* (New Brunswick, NJ: Rutgers University Press: 2009); Marcia J. Bunge, Terence Fretheim, and Beverly Roberts Gaventa, eds., *The Child in the Bible* (Grand Rapids: Eerdmans, 2008); and Marcia J. Bunge, ed., *The Child in Christian Thought* (Grand Rapids: Eerdmans, 2001).
2. I have written extensively about these six central perspectives in several articles about robust theologies of childhood. See, for example, Marcia J. Bunge, "The Dignity and Complexity of Children: Constructing Christian Theologies of Childhood," in *Nurturing Child and Adolescent Spirituality: Perspectives from the World's Religious Traditions*, edited by Karen Marie Yust, Aostre N. Johnson, Sandy Eisenberg Sasso, and Eugene C. Roehlkepartain, (Lanham, MA: Rowman and Littlefield, 2006) 43-68; Marcia J. Bunge, "A More Vibrant Theology of Children," *Christian Reflection: A Series in Faith and Ethics* (Summer, 2003): 11-19; Marcia J. Bunge, "Retrieving a Biblically Informed View of Children: Implications for Religious Education, a Theology of Childhood, and Social Justice," *Lutheran Education* 139, no. 2 (Winter 2003): 72-87; and Marcia J. Bunge, "The Child, Religion, and the Academy: Developing Robust Theological and Religious Understandings of Children and Childhood," *Journal of Religion* 86. no. 4 (October, 2006): 549-578.
3. An additional text related to this theme is when Leah, Jacob's first wife, speaks of her sixth son as a dowry, or wedding gift, presented by God (Gen 30:20). Several biblical passages indicate that parents who receive these precious gifts are

being "remembered" by God (Gen 30:22; 1 Sam 1:11, 19) and given "good fortune" (Gen 30:11). To be "fruitful"—have many children—is to receive God's blessing. The Psalmist says children are a "heritage" from the Lord and a "reward" (Ps 127:3).

4. Johannes Amos Comenius, *The School of Infancy* (1663), edited and introduced by Ernest M. Eller (Chapel Hill: The University of North Carolina Press, 1956), 59-70. The ideas of Comenius (1592-1670 C.E.) are influential far beyond the church, and he is often called the "father of modern education." His popular book, *The School of Infancy*, points out the complex sensibilities and development of infants and young children and the need to nurture them at a very young age.

5. Cyprian, Letter 64.3; in *Letters*, translated by Sister Rose Bernard Donna (Washington, D.C: Catholic University of America Press, 1964), 217-218. Although Cyprian is making strong claims for the spiritual and divine equality of children, he does not draw implications for their social equality.

6. See, for example, John Chrysostom, *On Marriage and Family Life*, translated by Catherine P. Roth and David Anderson (New York: St. Vladimir's Seminary Press, 1986).

7. Martin Luther, *Luther's Large Catechism*, translated by F. Samuel Janzow (St. Louis: Concordia, 1978), 40.

8. Martin Luther, *Luther's Works*, edited by Jaroslav Pelikan and Helmut Lehmann (St. Louis: Concordia, 1955-1986), 45:386.

7.

Whatever Happened to Inclusivity?

LESLIE NEUGENT

Leslie Neugent is an ordained minister in the United Church of Christ and serves at Wayzata Community Church in Minnesota. In 2012, she launched a radically inclusive worship service and ministry called Parables. Leslie is author of *Red Fish Theology: A How-To Guide for Offering a Radically Inclusive Worship Service with the Special Needs Community.*

The Church has done harm.

That's a pretty bold statement, isn't it? But it's true. I don't mean your church, or my church, or the church down the street. I mean The Church. Universal. All of us. We want to be inclusive. We want to show *agape* love, to love unconditionally. We want to believe that "all are welcome" in our midst. But we just can't always seem to pull it off. When we are confronted with the *xenos* – the "other," the stranger, the alien, the one who doesn't fit nicely into our tight little box of "acceptability" – we circle the wagons and sometimes brazenly, but more often subtly, whisper, "Sorry, my friend, it turns out there's no room at the inn."

I'd argue we are guilty of this kind of exclusion with all sorts of folk who are deemed "different" from us. But I am the mother of a 21-year-old son with Down syndrome; he is severely developmentally disabled, non-verbal, and medically complex. And I have had a front-row seat to the blatant and not-so-blatant rejection that those who are cognitively different – those with developmental disabilities – experience in our sacred places of worship. It's safe to say that families like ours are flat-out not welcome.

Why? Because, like my son, many of these children and adults with special needs can come with significant challenges. Many don't sit well in rows of seats facing forward, or can't follow the rules for when they can talk and when they must sit quietly to listen. Many need to move around a space; some who are nonverbal need to vocalize, which to the outside world can sound a lot like yelling or disruptive groaning. It's not that they *won't* fit in. Many *cannot* fit in, and so their God-given gifts are left at the door. And *we are the lesser for it.*

A Call to Radical Inclusivity

A few years ago, I had a eureka moment about this. I realized what harm the church is actually doing to families with special needs children, and how much *we* are missing when we avoid, neglect, or reject the "stranger." I was in my final year of seminary and was getting ready to be ordained as a minister in the United Church of Christ. I was poised to be a hospital chaplain and was anxious to get going on what had felt like my "divine call" for over a decade. I had been clear in my discernment that I *did not* want to work with the community of folks with disabilities. I had been very clear. I live in that reality every day with my son and I had no interest in making it a career. But God had other plans.

It was a regular Sunday morning at my church in Wayzata, Minnesota, when a boy named Kevin, who has spina bifida, was wheeled down the aisle of the sanctuary in his small wheelchair. His father found a seat just as the senior minister began to give his sermon.

Now, one thing you need to know is that this is a large sanctuary with seating for well over 800 people! I know from experience that when you preach from the pulpit in this massive space all you can hear is your own voice echoing from every wall. The other thing you need to know is that this was during what I call our formal "bells and smells" service, complete with a robed choir, symphony instruments, and strict but unspoken rules of "appropriate behaviour."

That's when it happened. Right there, in the middle of the sermon in this formal space, Kevin broke into song. "Jesus loves me this I know, for the Bible tells me so!"

We don't do this sort of thing during our traditional bells and smells service! We don't do anything that isn't part of the pre-determined order of service in the bulletin – or at least we try very hard not to! So this unanticipated singing seemed appalling. The room immediately felt awkward and people turned and stared as Kevin's dad bolted into action. Kevin and his wheelchair went flying up the aisle and out of the space in a flash so that all would be as it "should be." And the minister never knew it even happened. It was all *that* fast.

I vividly remember watching this moment unfold, and I thought to myself, "My God, *that* was the holiest moment of the hour! How did we miss it?" Jesus said, "Let the little children come to me," and we blew it. The Holy Spirit was blowing mightily and we shoved it right back into the neat little box of the formal service that we had constructed.

That's when I saw my years of working toward a chaplaincy career careen into a sharp left turn. That's the moment I heard a new call, the call to dive headlong into a ministry of empowerment for children and adults with special needs. The call was loud and clear. It was a call for us to be like Jesus; a call to turn the world upside down, to be brazen and radical in our inclusivity. It was a call to flip the paradigm of how we view ministering to the disabled. It was a call to move from viewing the cognitively disabled as a charity to be served, to seeing them as a spiritually-gifted community who could *teach us*. And it was a call to help other churches do the same. It's not what I had planned to do with my life, but as you might have experienced yourself, the Spirit was a-blowin' and it was time to hang on and enjoy the ride.

The Birth of a Ministry

This Holy Moment with Kevin started with a simple song. A song with a message that each of us needs to hear each and every day: "Jesus loves me, this I know." And yet, our rules and human-made blinders kept us from hearing it. That moment was a great reminder to us, the church, that *everyone* is needed to complete the body of Christ. Remember what the apostle Paul tells the people of Corinth in 1 Corinthians 12 about how every single person has a role to play in order to show us who God is:

> *Everyone gets in on it, everyone benefits ... all kinds of things are handed out by the Spirit to all kinds of people. The variety is wonderful...wise counsel, clear understanding, simple trust, healing the sick, miraculous acts, proclamation, discernment, and tongues.*
> (Eugene Peterson's *The Message*)

Did you hear what Paul said? *Everyone* gets in on it. *Everyone* has a gift to share. Everyone means everyone, no exceptions! This seemed like a good place to begin a ministry celebrating the gifts that people with disabilities offer the rest of us. Because the bottom line is that the body of Christ is not complete without them.

So a ministry called *Parables* was born.

We chose the name *Parables* because it best describes this community. Just like Jesus' parables in the Bible, our community of folks with cognitive disabilities turns the world upside down. Just like Jesus' parables, these folks offer profound lessons that are hard to hear. They challenge the status quo, and they are teachers of unpopular things – "Jesusy things" as Anne Lamott says – such as humility, vulnerability, dependence, and honesty.

When I was in seminary, I had to write a paper for a capstone class on constructive theology. In it I described my son, JJ, as the greatest parable of my life. My professor was intrigued by my choice of words and he responded by saying, "I am surprised that you didn't call him a blessing." I smiled and said, "Oh no, my son is way more complicated than a blessing. He is a teacher of hard lessons that I would rather not learn. He is my parable."

Our logo for *Parables* says it all in one simple picture. It consists of a school of fish swimming in one direction and then one lone red fish swimming the opposite way. It's not swimming the *wrong* way, just a *different* way. And that is us, the *Parables* community. We are the red fishes who swim the *other* way. And I would argue that Jesus was a red fish as well. Jesus and his followers shook things up. They swam against the current of the times. They upset the status quo. And it changed the world.

Ministry Nuts and Bolts

WHAT AND WHO PARABLES IS

Parables is a Sunday morning worship service that celebrates the unique gifts people with special needs have to offer the world. We invite everyone to come exactly as they are. We invite those with cognitive disabilities, and those with social/emotional/behavioural challenges. And we invite their families.

But it's much more challenging and radical than it seems, because when we say, "Come as you are," we really have to mean it. The families who participate in *Parables* have been harmed by their communities, schools, and even churches. So if they come in the door, they come in anxious and fearful, suspicious and guarded. I often compare our community of families with special needs to a group of mice: we live in a subterranean culture that stays underground and out of sight because it's often too hard and too painful to come out. So when we do come to the surface, we sniff things out to find out if the space is safe. Will our child and our family be welcomed, loved, and missed if we are not there? And if we get a whiff of judgment, back into the hole we go. And we will tell all the rest of the mice to stay away, because it just isn't safe.

In order for us to stay a "safe" place for our families, we implement only two rules each Sunday morning. First: nobody gets hurt physically. Second: nobody gets hurt emotionally. Whatever else might happen in that space, we love each other through it.

We also invite others from the wider congregation and the community at large to come and join us, to experience and learn from the profound connection that the *Parables* community has to the unbridled power of the Holy Spirit. We make a point of naming the fact that we hold our services in a separate space – not as an act of segregation, but as an act of deliberate empowerment. The members of our community want to be who they are uniquely created to be – *without apology*. So worshipping in a safe place, one where we don't have to worry so much about keeping hymnals in their places and staying in our seats, is imperative. We welcome any and all to join with us as we each boldly live into our God-given gifts.

WHY WE HAVE PARABLES

Take a close look at who Jesus hung around with during his short time of ministry on earth. He spent his time with the castaways – those perceived to be outcasts, and those who lived on the margins of society. Jesus was not found hobnobbing with elite scholars or the swanky country club set. He got to know the lepers, the sick, the tax collectors, the broken, the maimed, and the rejected.

In the Gospel of John, Jesus prays that his disciples would live *in* the world but not be *of* it, saying,

> *I have given them your word, and the world has hated them because they do not belong to the world, just as I do not belong to the world. I am not asking you to take them out of the world, but I ask you to protect them from the evil one. They do not belong to the world, just as I do not belong to the world. Sanctify them in the truth; your word is truth. As you have sent me into the world, so I have sent them into the world. And for their sakes I sanctify myself, so that they also may be sanctified in truth* (Jn 17:14-19).

Although his prayer is more cryptic than the oft-quoted warning to "be *in* the world but not *of* the world," the nuance here is important if we are serious about being true disciples of Jesus. It tells us that following

Jesus will be unpopular. In John 15, Jesus goes so far as to say that we who live in the way of Jesus will be *hated* by the world. Two thousand years ago when Jesus was at the height of his ministry, the Jews were looking out for a mighty king who would ride into town on a powerful stallion and lead them with worldly strength. And instead, Jesus, a local carpenter's son, showed up on a lowly donkey in simple clothes and dirty sandals and declared bombshells like these:

Blessed are the meek.
The first shall be last and the last shall be first.
Invite everyone to the table—the poor, the crippled, the blind, the lame.
Love your enemies.
Go and sell all you have and give to the poor.
Forgive seventy times seven times.
Turn the other cheek.
When someone takes your coat, offer them your shirt.
Pray for those who persecute you.
Visit the imprisoned.
To save your life you must lose it.
Take up your cross and follow me.

These were highly unpopular mandates from Jesus. They were radically challenging and disarmingly uncomfortable directives that continue to rock the world and upset the status quo. Jesus was telling us that if we truly follow him we will never *fit* in the world around us. We are destined to be *misfits*.

So it's not surprising that in Eugene Peterson's translation of the apostle Paul's words to the "holier-than-thou" people of Corinth, Paul makes the important observation that "it seems to me that God has put us who bear his Message on stage in a theatre in which no one wants to buy a ticket. We're something everyone stands around and stares at, like an accident in the street. We're the Messiah's misfits."[1]

The Oxford Dictionary defines the term *misfit* as "a person whose behaviour or attitude sets them apart from others in an uncomfortably conspicuous way." Some synonyms of the word are *non-conformist*, *eccentric*, and *maverick*. Jesus was a misfit. He was a red fish who swam in the opposite direction to those around him. And Paul called himself and the other apostles "the Messiah's misfits." So there's a theological and historical precedent to being a misfit. And maybe there is something we can learn from the people the world rejects. Theologically speaking, people with cognitive disabilities have a lot to teach us about this call to be *in* the world but not *of* it. It's how they live their very lives, day in and day out. They are the quintessential Messiah's misfits. And it would be wise for us to pay attention to their gifts.

Sometime during all the effort it took to start a *Parables* ministry – a place where the Messiah's misfits can come just as they are – I realized that having such a ministry isn't just a theologically sound thing to do. It is also a smart thing to do. Right now, for the most part, mainline Protestant churches are on the decline, with many denominations closing the doors of once-thriving congregations on a regular basis. And at the very same time, the diagnosis of autism spectrum disorder has been rising dramatically, with the most recent Center for Disease Control report announcing that one out of every 68 children is being diagnosed with this condition every year.[2] This is a staggering number that we should stop and pay attention to.

These shocking statistics mark a game-changing opportunity for churches. While many of our congregations are declining in attendance, a burgeoning group of families with children who live on the autism spectrum need a loving and supportive spiritual home.[3] What's more, this community has spiritual gifts we just can't find anywhere else. This is a holy moment in time that should not be ignored. It's an all-round win-win. But we need to be ready for it.

THE WHEN AND WHERE OF PARABLES

When I share the work of *Parables*, often someone says, "We have a service like *Parables* at our church." While their efforts are admirable, I must admit that I have yet to find such a statement to be true. Yes, many churches offer a periodic worship service for the special needs community, perhaps once or twice a month, and usually on a Wednesday or a Sunday night in a basement or all-purpose room. But this is not the *Parables* model.

Our 45-minute *Parables* worship service is offered at 10:30 *every* Sunday morning in our congregation's chapel – a sacred space of worship within the church – with food and fellowship offered after each service. Both the time and place of our service say a lot about the theological import of this community. In our church, we think it is imperative that the community of people with special needs worship *when* and *where* the rest of the congregation does. Time and space matters. Meeting during "prime church time" in a sacred space communicates clearly that the *Parables* community is valued, and is necessary in order to complete the body of Christ. It says that the party wouldn't be complete without them.

THE DESIGN OF PARABLES

When we started *Parables*, we designed the worship service *with* and not *for* the families with special needs children. Their partnership has been crucial at every step. Our bulletin is a simple two-sided card with the flow of the service and the words to the prayers included in large print. The bulletin looks identical every week except for changes in the words of the responsive prayer. We honour the fact that routine and consistency are important to this community. We try to keep the pace and rhythm of the morning the same from week to week so our congregants feel comfortable and know what to expect.

What's most important is that the members of the *Parables* community are the stars of the show at every service. Each Sunday morning, our folks with developmental disabilities are leaders. They welcome people to the space. They march, dance, and roll into the chapel playing instruments and singing, "When the Saints Go Marching In." They lead the procession out of the space singing, "This Little Light of Mine." They say and read the prayers and scripture from the pulpit. They lead the songs from the altar, collect the offering, and pray over Communion with me. They offer the benediction. And sometimes they preach! For

45 minutes each week, they are held tightly by a community of 70 to over 100 people and encouraged to boldly live into who God created them to be. This is what empowerment looks like. This is what the Church is called to be and do.

An ethos of generosity is pervasive in the *Parables* worship space. If our scripture reader has trouble with reading skills or stutters, we sit back and patiently wait or offer support when needed. Time is not important here – love is. When we take a deep breath and let the Spirit move in the room, something profoundly holy happens. The sermon breaks out all over the place, and not just from the pulpit. It's in the hugs being offered non-stop throughout the room. It's in watching the shyest child in the space come to the altar to lay their head on our resident therapy dog, Getty. It's in the songs about Jesus being sung when nobody else is singing. At *Parables,* if you are paying attention, the ministry is all around you. The gospel is proclaimed in unexpected and never-ending ways! This community cannot help themselves: they are spiritual masters. If the congregation hears my message from the pulpit, that's a bonus. But even if they don't, when they leave *Parables* worship they know that they have been touched deeply by the Spirit of God.

Music is integral to *Parables*. There is compelling research out there to support the fact that music is of special import to people who have cognitive disabilities.[4] It is the language of the soul. During our worship service, we sing often and keep the songs simple and familiar so everyone can join in. We modulate the pace of the songs from upbeat and lively to quiet and reflective to ensure that our congregants don't get over-stimulated.

You may be wondering how on earth one gets a ministry like this up and running. My best advice is to be patient and not go it alone. When we started this ministry, it was imperative to find a small group of parents who have children with developmental disabilities to team up with. We started with a support group of five couples who together developed a deep trust in one another over a couple of years. We dreamed together about what a ministry for our kids might look like. We developed the worship service bulletin together and had dress rehearsals with our core group of families to get comfortable in the flow and atmosphere that we were trying to achieve. By the time we opened the service up to the public we had a firm anchor of trust amongst us so that we could be fully welcoming to whomever came through the door. This preparation and trust-building is crucial because many of these families are afraid to bring their children into a new space for fear of being judged or rejected. Our group was prepared and ready to welcome others to come *exactly* as they are...*no exceptions*. And that has made all the difference. That's radical inclusivity.

A Few Final Words

I began this chapter with a blunt statement that the church has done harm. We have failed to live into Jesus' call to be truly inclusive in our love. Oh sure, we've gotten it right at times. But I stand firm in my belief that the church has missed the mark of true inclusivity. We have become safe little places of "alikeness" that fail to live into the radical love and openness to difference that Jesus modelled so well.

Parables is one effort to right the course of the ship, to make good on Jesus' call to love without bounds, to recognize the gifts that each and every person who is "fearfully and wonderfully made" has to share. The apostle Paul is clear about this – we need everyone present at the table to be the full body of Christ. *Everyone means everyone.*

A few years ago I attended the annual Accessibility Conference in Washington DC and had the privilege of hearing Tim Shriver speak about his family's work in starting Special Olympics. He shared about how this organization has profoundly changed lives by offering a platform from which people with developmental disabilities can find their gifts and celebrate their accomplishments. The organization has had a direct role in building self-esteem and confidence in folks that rarely get opportunities to be counted and valued. I recently also had the opportunity to visit with Tim's brother, Anthony Shriver, who leads an organization called Best Buddies, an offshoot of Special Olympics that pairs people with disabilities with "neuro-typical" college-age friends. Friendship is another area that is often lost to those with special needs. Loneliness and isolation are common themes in the lives of these folks, and programs like Best Buddies are changing that.

So all this leads me to ask: *Where is the church?* If secular organizations like Special Olympics and Best Buddies have broken new ground and led the way of radical inclusivity that Jesus so clearly calls us, his disciples, to do, *where are we?* The church has been left in the dust, more concerned about buildings and budgets, power and privilege, than extending – and receiving! – radical hospitality from those our society pushes to the margins. This needs to change. This must change if we are truly to call ourselves disciples of the most radically inclusive one of all. It's time to get busy. We have a lot to do.[5]

1.   Eugene Peterson, *The Message.* 1 Cor 4:9 (Peabody MA: Navpress Publishing Group, 2002)..

2.   "Autism Spectrum Disorder (ASD)," *Center for Disease Control and Prevention*, updated July 11, 2016, accessed December 19, 2017, https://www.cdc.gov/ncbddd/autism/data.html.

3.   For an excellent chapter about youth ministry and the Autism Spectrum, see Dixon Kinser, "Jesus on the Autism Spectrum," in *Faith Forward: A Dialogue about Children, Youth, and a New Kind of Christianity*, edited by David M. Csinos and Melvin Bray. (Kelowna, BC: CopperHouse, 2013), 213-23.

4.   See, for example, Sudha M. Srinivasan and Anjana N. Bhat, "A Review of 'Music and Movement' Therapies for Children with Autism: Embodied Instruments for Multisystem Development," *Frontiers in Integrative Neuroscience* 7, no. 22 (2013), accessed December 19, 2017, https://www.frontiersin.org/articles/10.3389/fnint.2013.00022/full.

5.   If you would like to see a *Parables* worship service in action, visit www.wayzatacommunitychurch.org, then go to the "*Parables* Special Needs Ministry" link. View the "*Parables* Worship Video" on that page.
     If you'd like more information about how to start your own *Parables* Ministry go to www.ucc.org, "Worship Resources," and type "Parables" in the search bar. That will take you to the link to purchase the How-To Guide.
     If you are interested in using the *Parables* worship and marketing materials that we have developed, go to www.wayzatacommunitychurch.org and go to the "*Parables* Special Needs Ministry" link, then go to the link that says, "Start a *Parables* Ministry at Your Church," and for a small donation you can have access to our complete kit of materials.

8.

Looking Back as a Parent

What Worked, What Didn't, and What I Hope Faith Forward Can Do

BRIAN D. MCLAREN

Brian D. McLaren is an author, speaker, activist, public theologian, and passionate advocate for "a new kind of Christianity." He is an Auburn Senior Fellow, a contributor to We Stand With Love, and a leader in the Convergence Network. His books include *The Great Spiritual Migration* and *We Make the Road by Walking*.

My wife, Grace, and I are blessed with four amazing kids. It seems like just yesterday that we were changing diapers and helping with science fair projects and paying college tuitions. We blinked twice, and suddenly they're 36, 35, 33, and 30. Two of them have kids of their own.

For many years in my roles as pastor and father, I had certain ideas about the spiritual formation of children and youth. But now, as a grandfather, I find my perspective changing. I have the amazing pleasure of watching my kids raise their kids in the context of all we taught them, and I see what my kids feel is worth imitating and what they feel worth leaving behind.

One of my daughters is a college professor, and it's very obvious that her daughter is a budding theologian. My granddaughter, who was just about to turn four at the time and didn't know how to write, took a pencil and scribbled on the paper and talked out loud about what she was "writing."

I did the same thing when I was about her age. I filled up books with scribbles. (Looking back, I suppose it was kind of like writing in tongues.) I remember wondering, "What am I saying?" But my granddaughter had a good sense of what she wanted to say. She started narrating her scribbles to the nanny looking after her. "Dear God, I have a few questions for you. Do you have a job, or do you just play?" I like that question!

Her next question was way beyond me: "Are the people who died with you in heaven already, or are all of us there and we just don't know it yet?" Not bad for an almost-four-year-old.

My son has two daughters, and his younger daughter was born quite prematurely, weighing in at two pounds. I remember the first time I held her, so frail and so delicate, her tiny hand seeming so perfect and so impossibly small. She spent a lot of time in the hospital as a little preemie, and in the following years, her doctors initiated early interventions to deal with signs of learning disabilities and autism. I watched my son and daughter-in-law cope with all of this, and I knew their hearts were getting bigger, opening to depths of love within them that they never knew they were capable of. And, of course, as a grandfather, I felt the same thing happening to me.

Looking Back: What Worked

When my wife and I were parents of small kids ourselves, the daily demands of dressing, cooking, cleaning, bathing, playing, correcting, teaching, waking up, putting to bed, breaking up arguments, pre-empting arguments, and all the other parenting activities were so demanding that we hardly had time to reflect on what we were doing. But now, as a grandfather, I have more time, more distance, and, I hope, more perspective. I'm at a good place to evaluate what worked and what didn't, what proved fruitful and what proved less so. Here are nine things that stand out as especially fruitful.

First, we made spirituality a natural part of the rhythms of our daily life. We prayed at meals. We prayed at bedtime. When joyful things happened, in moments of awe and delight, Grace and I spoke of our gratitude to God; when painful, difficult things happened, we stopped and prayed. Our kids saw this, and it seems to have "stuck."

Because our preemie granddaughter had some developmental issues when she was younger, for quite a while she never played with anybody, not even her sister. She would occupy herself, but other people seemed of no interest to her. (It's completely different now, thanks be to God.) In the middle of that time, my son came home from work one day and saw his two daughters playing together. Nothing special for many families, but for my son it was a moment of ecstasy. He texted me a photo of the two of them sitting next to each other on the floor, playing with toys, and he included these words: "Dad, I wondered if I'd ever see this in my whole life. Life is good, and God is good." And it struck me that this instinct to refer the experiences of life to God was still with my son; I believe it will stay with his children too.

A second element of our spiritual formation efforts that has proven fruitful is this: we connected God with acts of service. My kids saw their parents try to serve other people and put themselves out for other people; now I watch my grandkids watching their parents doing the same thing, and I realize that when faith is expressed in acts of service, it sticks. It stays with them.

Third, we tried to share our own spiritual struggles with our kids, including our own unanswered theological questions and spiritual challenges. We would ask our kids to pray for us when we were going through a hard time, and we would tell them about our own doubts. As a result, they felt free to do the same.

One Sunday, for example, one of my sons, then about six years old, stayed to the bitter end of all the church activities that I, as a pastor, had to be involved with. As we were driving home, with just the two of us in the car, I said, "So, how was your Sunday school class today?"

He said, "Oh Dad, I don't want to go into it."

"What's wrong?" I asked. I felt like he was apologizing to me, that he felt I'd be really disappointed to hear what they talked about in a Sunday school class at my church.

"Well, today it was really far-fetched."

I thought, *a six year old, far-fetched – where did you get that vocabulary?* I asked, "What happened?"

And he said, "Dad, they tried to tell us about some bunch of people who came to an ocean and it opened up and they walked through on dry ground. Can you believe it?" He looked thoroughly disgusted. That didn't say a lot about my success in teaching him the Exodus story by the age of six, but it did say a lot about his freedom to express his honest reactions to stories from the Bible.

That leads to a fourth element of spiritual formation that seems to have clicked and worked for our kids. We treated them as young but legitimate members of the interpretive community. When our kids came to us with their questions, Grace and I would often ask, "What do you think? What do you think that could mean?" In that way, we tried to honour their voices, their thoughts, their imaginations, their insights, and their misgivings. It's fascinating now to watch my little grandkids show themselves as budding young theologians. They feel they have a voice as bona fide members of the interpretive community, and they have their own thoughts and questions about God, just as their parents and grandparents did.

Of course, the key to this was avoiding judgement, which is a fifth element of what we did that has proven fruitful. I recall the night one of my daughters, when she was about 15, said, "Dad, I have something I need to talk to you about in private. Can you come down to my room?"

When a 15-year-old daughter says that she wants to talk in private, any parent is likely to experience a little atrial fibrillation. As I entered her room, I was thinking, *Okay, prepare yourself. This could be about ...anything.*

Then she pointed to the bed. "Sit down on the bed," she said. And I'm thinking, *Yikes. This seems serious.* She stood in front of me, looking a little bit like an attorney standing in front of a jury. *Prepare for the worst*, I said to myself.

My daughter looked terribly serious. She took a deep breath. I swallowed hard, and she spoke. "Dad, you believe in evolution, don't you?"

I said, "Well yeah, I think evolution is one of God's coolest creations."

And she said, "Dad, I don't believe in evolution."

Now at that moment, I felt...well, you can imagine how I felt. I was relieved, almost giddy. And I knew exactly what had happened. Our congregation had hired a somewhat fundamentalist youth worker, and I realized that the youth worker was trying to straighten the church out by telling the teens that the pastor was a heretic. That put my daughter in a tough situation, since I was that heretical pastor! So she was telling me that she was siding with the youth pastor, which struck me as terribly sweet because she knew that I would accept her if she didn't agree with me, and I don't think that the youth pastor would have. The fact that she knew that she could disagree with her pastor/author/speaker/dad and it would be okay...that was so important.

Sixth, we surrounded our kids with a faith community. When I hear my adult kids talk about what it was like growing up in a pastor's family, even though it had a few downsides they recall it overall as a great blessing. It surrounded them with wonderful people and a wide circle of friends. Hospitality was the norm for them. That meant welcoming into our home all kinds of people from church, but it also meant welcoming people who were atheists, people of other religions, people with various life-controlling problems. And whoever they were, our guests were loved and respected. After September 11, 2001, I became good friends with an Imam from a mosque down the road. He was from Pakistan, and was not into technology or cell phones. So if he wanted to talk to me, he would always show up at church. And I remember my daughter running up to me one Sunday morning and saying, "Hey Dad, your Imam is here!"

And you know, that wide sense of hospitality was a good thing – it stuck. I watch my kids opening their doors and hearts to people wherever they go, creating spaces of hospitality and community. And I'm quite certain their kids will be doing the same long after I'm gone.

Seventh, being part of a Christian community introduced my children to new experiences as well as new friends. My kids went places they never would have gone otherwise. They got involved in projects they otherwise never would have been involved with. Church life really was a wonderful avenue into new experiences, and I'm so glad that the kind of church they grew up in was the opposite of a "can't-don't-won't" church; it was a place of permission-giving, challenge, exploration, and adventure.

Eighth, we made sure to have fun. We took great vacations. We laughed a lot. We had good parties. We enjoyed life. And that wasn't in spite of our spirituality; it was an expression of it.

Last, but certainly not least, we didn't hide our mistakes. For example, when we were grouchy and sharp with our kids, when we didn't treat them with the respect they deserved, we'd apologize. That has continued even since they've grown up. In recent years I've come to terms with some of the long-term negative effects of my own fundamentalist upbringing, effects that had a negative impact on my parenting. So I've had a talk with my kids who are now parents, and I've said, "I want to tell you some of the things I did as a parent that I really regret. I'm really, really sorry." They said, "No, don't beat yourself up Dad." But I told them I needed to apologize, for my own sake as well as theirs.

Looking Back: What Didn't Work

That brings me to the elements that backfired, the elements of spiritual formation that I regret using in my parenting years. Most seriously, I regret the degree to which my children were exposed to fundamentalism without sufficient warning. Even though I had left the fundamentalism of my upbringing behind, our kids were exposed to it through relatives and friends and other connections, and we didn't adequately prepare them for its negative effects. Sure, my daughter got over the fundamentalism of that youth worker who convinced her to become (temporarily) a literal six-day creationist. But other damage was done that has been more long-lasting. At summer camp, for example, some of my kids were exposed to "purity" rhetoric that caused them a lot of anxiety about their sexuality. I wish I had been able to pre-empt that harm.

Growing up in our home, when our kids heard the word *Christian*, by and large it meant something positive, something life-giving, something wise and wonderful. But I remember when one of my sons started college and said, "I hate to tell you this, Dad, but the word *Christian* doesn't mean at my campus what it means here. It means something very different." I wish I'd prepared my children more for that wide diversity of what is held under the one term *Christian*.

Similarly, I wish that I had been more overt about how we interpreted the Bible – critically, post-critically, and literarily, rather than pre-critically and literally. And I wish I'd been bolder in general about being different, both with my family and in my church. I wish I had said, "Look, we're not just trying to form you in the same old same old. We're really trying to do something fresh and different here." I think I minimized that with both my kids and my church, and I think that was a mistake.

A Request (Actually, Six of Them)

So, that's some of what I feel worked and didn't work in my own life as a parent. My experience makes me want to make six requests, not only of parents but also of faith leaders, practitioners, children's ministers, and youth workers who are thinking about the spiritual formation of my grandchildren's generation.

A CURRICULUM OF LOVE

First, I hope you will help to create a curriculum of love.[1] I have it on very good authority that you can speak with the tongues of men and of angels, and if you have not love, it's not worth much. And I have it on very good authority that you can have the correct doctrines, you can have the correct practices, on a Sunday morning you can do all the right rituals in the right order, and you can believe the right thing about the Pope or the Bible or whatever, but if you don't have love, it's not worth much (1 Cor 13:1-3).

I have been re-reading the letters of Paul lately, noticing what an incredibly daring and dangerous person he was to say things such as (Gal 5:6), "Neither circumcision nor uncircumcision matters at all. The only thing that matters is faith, expressing itself in love." That's a radical statement! So I think we actually have to get serious as we never have before. We need to ask questions like these: "What is a kid capable of learning about love by the age of four? And by the age of eight? And by the age of 12? And by the age of 16? And how can we develop age-appropriate ways of teaching this curriculum of love?"

It strikes me as funny that we don't let people drive a car without learning how to make a left-hand turn and how to parallel park, but we let people who don't have a clue about basic communication skills get married, and we let people who don't have a clue about basic parenting skills have kids, and we let people who don't have a clue about basic teamwork skills run corporations. If love is the heart of the Christian message, isn't it about time that Christians develop a basic curriculum of love? For neighbour, for stranger, outsider, outcast, enemy? For oneself? For the earth? And for God?[2]

Sometimes I think we shouldn't even mention God until we've taught children the basics about how to love their neighbour, and how to love themselves, and how to love a stranger, and how to love the earth. I say this because of something that's written in the New Testament (1 Jn 4:7-8): "Beloved, let us love one another, for love is of God; and everyone who loves is born of God and knows God. Whoever does not love does not know God, for God is love."

If we taught children and youth how to love neighbour, other, self, and the earth, and then we talked about God, I like to think that they'd say, "Oh, I already know about God," or, "Ah. That makes perfect sense," because in the act of loving they would have already experienced God. But what do we do instead? We teach young people all of these abstract ideas that they're supposed to understand and affirm about God. Let's tell the truth: lots of us adults don't understand those abstract ideas. And lots of us understand them but don't actually think they're accurate or honest. That's why I think we need to begin our curriculum of love not with abstractions but with practice. In the practice of love, God becomes more than an invisible abstraction to which one gives mental assent.

A CURRICULUM OF GOD

Along with a curriculum of love, I hope that a new generation of Christian practitioners and parents can work on a curriculum of God that incorporates what one of my mentors says: You should teach children about God the way you teach them about sex – answer their questions honestly, but never say anything to them now that you'll have to contradict later on.

In the same way, when we teach young people about God we need to say, "I'm going to tell you this, but there's a lot more to it than what I'm saying now. There's more than I have even begun to understand." I often think that whatever adjectives we use to describe God, we have to add *er* onto the word. God is great, but actually God is *greater* than I understand. God is good, but actually God is *better* than I understand.

Whatever shape our curriculum of God takes, it should always just reaffirm that there's more to God than any of us understand, and that's why God is the most important and fascinating subject in the universe.

A CURRICULUM OF CONTEMPLATION

Third, I hope a new generation of Christian practitioners with young people can help develop a curriculum of contemplation, for the development of the inner life. Older folks often forget that little children have stress. They have heartbreak. They have trauma. And, of course, older children and teenagers do too. And there are invaluable resources in our broad Christian tradition, precious resources in the scriptures, to help us strengthen the inner life in order to deal with stress, heartbreak, and trauma.

We talk a lot about guilt in traditional Christian theology, but I've had some experiences in the past couple of years where other people heaped shame on me. I was immediately taken back to junior high school, the petri dish in which the germs of a lifetime of shame foment.

And I realized that nobody in the Christian community helped me much with shame. Shame, and learning to identify, process, and shed it, is a huge dimension of the inner life. There are not a lot of places or resources that aim to help children, teens, or their parents with shame, loss, fear, anxiety, and other unavoidable elements of the inner life. Our faith communities could be incredible resources if people like us would break out of our ruts and do some creative experimentation.

A CURRICULUM OF JUSTICE, GENEROSITY, AND ACTION

Fourth, I hope that parents, and children's and youth ministry leaders can together develop a curriculum of justice, generosity, and action so that we can promise that *every child who grows up in our faith community will be trained as a life-long activist for justice and for peace and for joy in the Holy Spirit.*

A few years ago I got to spend some time with some members of the Catholic Student Movement. This movement is not very well known in the United States, but in certain parts of the world the Catholic Student Movement is quite powerful on university campuses. And they have a clear and very positive agenda for you as a freshman; they don't just want you to go to Mass and not have an abortion. They have an agenda for you. By the time you graduate from university, they want you to become a life-long activist in the Catholic tradition of social justice. They've got four years to work on you, and they know what they want to teach you to understand and see and do. That's what we need in the church more broadly.

We need to face the facts. Many forces in our world are trying to shape our children. For example, Fox News is trying to raise our kids with a political agenda set by corporations and political manipulators. Every time they turn on a screen and they get advertisements, there's a whole economic agenda that's being enforced. As parents and leaders, we need to say, "If you're part of this faith community, we want to teach you how to exegete advertisements that are trying to spiritually malform you. We want to teach you to exegete political arguments that are trying to malform you. We want to spiritually form you, and so we have to help you see the opposition. That's our agenda, and we're overt and serious about it." We need to have a curriculum of justice, generosity, and action that is honest enough to tell this to our young people.

A CURRICULUM OF COMMUNITY

I also hope a new generation of parents and leaders can find ways to promote earlier involvement in Christian community life. I know a lot of churches have special events like Youth Sunday and Children's Service. These may be good practices, but if we are honest, we need to admit that they are not good enough. What we need is to make every Sunday a Youth Sunday, every service a Children's Service.

I attend a little Episcopal church on a small island in south-west Florida. Our rector loves children and youth with diverse abilities. If you were to visit my church, you'd probably be surprised, and perhaps uncomfortable, with what happens during the service. For example, when the priest says, "The Lord be with you," and everybody responds, "And also with you," there's a young woman with Down syndrome who responds with more enthusiasm than anybody. Because of her condition, "And also with you," comes out as an incomprehensible yet very loud "Aauauuuuauuuaauh." Everybody in the congregation is used to it, and we hardly notice it. When the Lord's Prayer comes, she's belting out the prayer, full bore, but not with intelligible English words. If you come to my church and it's time for the offering, you might see some children with diverse abilities passing the offering baskets. You'll discover, as I did, how so-called disabled people can be so naturally included as partners and even leaders in public worship. It turns out they're pretty able, and in many ways exemplary!

We have no idea what could happen if we truly acted as if fourth graders, third graders, and sixth graders were not the church of tomorrow but the church of today. What would come about if we didn't include them just because they're cute or it's trendy to do so, but because we really respect them as members of the community? They have serious work to do, and we ought to value it more here than any place else in our culture. Think what would happen if we invited children to join us in mission, if we consulted teens in decision-making, if we celebrated young people for good work, just like we do everyone else. It would turn out that they're pretty able, and exemplary!

I was invited to speak at an Episcopal diocesan convention in Pennsylvania. These conventions used to be quite boring, with endless motions and votes and financial reports and so on. But this one diocese decided to turn things around. They handled the business in the least amount of time possible and then spent the rest of the time honouring people. There were awards for this and honours for that. It was like a festival of appreciation and celebration. And the high point of the whole convention was the special award for student activists. Some of the student recipients of this award were Episcopalians, but others were Jewish and Methodists who had been invited to the convention in order to be honoured. This sort of inclusion and honour is how it should be, and it is how it shall be if we dare to make it so.

A CURRICULUM OF BOLDNESS

Finally, I would hope that we would stop walking on eggshells and walk forward in boldness and courage. There is a major discontinuity between the church of the past and the church of the future, and it's time to stop denying and lamenting it. It's time to cross the bridge and get on with life on the other side. Most people know this and are ready for big changes. They're even for hungry for them. The emergence and convergence that many of us have been predicting is actually happening all around us. It's overdue, in fact. The cat's out of the bag. The memo is out. The future will be different from the past. So I wish we could pick a date, say, tomorrow or the day after that, and announce: "As of today, we're doing a new thing...starting with children and youth."

Through all of this, of course, I hope people will have fun and be good to one another and feel great about this creative new day we're part of. If you are an innovator in children's and youth ministry, I hope you realize that you are a hero surrounded by heroes. You are a creative genius surrounded by other creative geniuses. You are a trailblazer surrounded by other trailblazers. You have all kinds of superpowers that you don't know about. You're a mutant. Many people don't understand you, but you're not alone. Through organizations like Faith Forward, you're linking up with other people who are also mutants, and so together you're the X-Men.

What you're doing is infinitely important. Imagine holding my little two-pound granddaughter and looking in her deep brown, wide-open eyes. You think, "What's ahead? What world will this child face?" They say the odds are that this little baby will live into the triple digits. And so you think, "What will the world be like in a hundred years? And what does it mean to infuse this precious little child with a spring of living water that will flow with aliveness through all her days until she has great-grandchildren of her own?" What could possibly be more important than that?

1. I have written about the importance of a curriculum of love in chapter 3 of my recent book, *The Great Spiritual Migration*. See Brian D. McLaren, *The Great Spiritual Migration: How the World's Largest Religion is Seeking a Better Way to Be Christian* (New York: Convergent, 2016), 50-67.
2. This is something I expand upon in my other chapter in this volume.

PART III

HOPE

9.

More Reason for Hope

Living into God's Alternative Future

IVY BECKWITH

Ivy Beckwith is Faith Formation Team Leader for the United Church of Christ. She is a speaker, consultant, and author. Her books include *Children's Ministry in the Way of Jesus* (with David Csinos), and *Postmodern Children's Ministry*. She holds degrees in English and Religious Education, and has held educational positions in churches throughout the United States.

For a long time I've believed that faith communities play an important role in the positive spiritual nurture and formation of their members. However, in the past I connected this role to a very individualized personal faith formation. I believed the faith community worked with God's Spirit to transform individuals. Then, when the church had created children, youth, and adults who loved God and lived in the way of Jesus, these people would band together to create a community that would transform the world and usher in the reign of God. In my mind, personal transformation came first; these individuals then formed a community; then the community would transform the world. And if it didn't change the world, at least there would be individuals who loved God and lived in the way of Jesus and who could be those proverbial lit candles in the darkness.

But in recent months, my thinking surrounding these assumptions has been challenged. Author and consultant Peter Block, in his book *Community: The Structure of Belonging*, says that I am wrong, and that the ideas I just fleshed out about cultural and spiritual transformation aren't how it really works. He says I've had it backward. Instead, personal – and ultimately cultural and spiritual – transformation happens when we create and live in communities of possibility. These communities generate hospitality and generosity. These communities focus on answering the question: "What can we create together?"

According to Block, this question is answered when, in our communities, we "allow ourselves to use the language of healing and relatedness and belonging without embarrassment...[built on] the citizens' willingness to own up to their contribution, to be humble, to choose accountability, and to have faith in their own capacity to make authentic promises to create the alternative future."[1] If only this were a descriptor of the church.

Stuck Communities

Now, sometimes it is easier to understand what these communities are all about by holding up examples of what they are not. Transformative communities of possibility are not "stuck communities."[2] Stuck communities are defined by their fears, their isolation, and their desire for retribution. According to Block, the overriding characteristic of a stuck community is the decision to broadcast all the reasons it has to be afraid.[3] This kind of community values systems over relationships.[4] For example, someone who needs help in a stuck community is seen as a communal liability, something that affects the bottom line of economic prosperity or requires a rise in the cost of the church health insurance policy. Stuck communities see the future as a problem to be solved rather than something to be determined by the collective whole. Stuck communities value predictability. They want to take as much uncertainly as possible out of the future and march forward with a strong sense of where they are going and how they will get there.[5] But, says Block, "the only way to make tomorrow predictable is to make it just like today."[6]

The current political situation of the United States – my home country and context – exemplifies the characteristics of a stuck community. Our elected officials sow fear and promote isolation and retribution during discussions of foreign policy and immigration. We, the citizens, are encouraged to fear what "they" will do if Iran or North Korea possesses a nuclear weapon, or if immigrants cross our borders illegally. Our leaders talk of retaliation to any perceived aggression: invade their country, bomb their cities, put them in jail, or deport them. We're told we need to build a wall. And what could possibly be more isolating than a wall? The debates around affordable healthcare paint those with pre-existing conditions as a drain on resources and work to convince those who are lucky enough to be healthy that they should not help to care for them.

This of course describes only one extreme side of these Not-So-United States of America. But the other side is likewise stuck. They're stuck in their fear and anxiety about reactions to more progressive policy discussions and the conventional wisdom about voter preferences. All these are indicators – from both the right and the left – of a society that is stuck. The United States is a nationwide community that values systems over people, gives reason after reason to fear the other, and seeks the same old solutions as it consistently reaches for an all-too-predictable future.

Likewise, stuckness pervades our local churches. In almost every denomination and Christian tradition it seems that churches are anxious about meeting budgets and paying bills. They're anxious about declining attendance and crumbling buildings. They are anxious about losing teens and young people. And all this anxiety causes churches to focus inward, circle the wagons, and huddle together for survival. They refuse to take risks, and they try to solve the problems they're facing by using the same old methods. Ultimately, this anxiety leads to a loss of hope. And when our churches lose hope – that's when we've really lost our children and youth.

Let me sum up so far. Stuck communities strive to solve problems by acting in predictable and familiar ways and eliminating the fear-inducing "theys" (immigrants, Muslims, older people, the pastor), while communities of possibility and transformation (particularly communities where God's Spirit lives) live into an alternative future where no one needs a nuclear weapon, where all are welcome everywhere, and where hope in God's abundant provision trumps anxiety and fear every time.

Communities of Possibility

So what are the compelling characteristics of communities of possibility, the communities that transform their members, their surrounding communities, and their worlds? Peter Block gives us six characteristics of what these communities look like.

Communities of Hospitality

First, these communities are hospitable and welcoming. They receive and entertain strangers or guests without thought of reward, and with kindness and generosity.[7] Much of the discussion I hear around the church's loss of young adults treats these people as a commodity. Churches want to have young adults in their midst for what they can provide. They desire them for what the young people contribute to the existing community: energy, resources, and children. But today's young adults can keenly sense duplicity, and they know when they are being played. If a church gives off any whiff of desiring them because of what they can offer the church, they'll run for the hills. Transformative communities of possibility don't welcome people because of what they bring – they welcome simply because welcoming all is what the reign of God and a life of faith are all about.

Communities of Accountability

Second, members of transformative communities of possibility hold themselves and each other accountable for the future they live into.[8] Each member of the community is responsible for making the desired future happen. They take ownership of themselves and their actions. This accountability and ownership manifests as a willingness to care for the well-being of the whole. For example, in Japan, care of children is seen as a collective community responsibility. Visitors to Japan will see children wearing bright yellow hats because this makes it easier for adults to look out for them. Contrast this with the United States, where children are too often viewed as private property and thought to be under constant threat from others.

The ownership and accountability lived by the people in transformative communities of possibility also include a willingness to give up on personal entitlement which, according to Block, means eliminating the question of "what's in it for me?"[9] For Block, ownership and accountability involve a willingness to acknowledge that we have participated in creating, through commission or omission, the conditions we wish to see changed; transformative community will be created the moment we decide to act as the creators of that alternative future, as the creators of what we and our communities can become.[10]

Communities of Generosity

Transformative communities of possibility are generous communities that see each member as a gift with a special role in creating the alternative future they envision, rather than a liability or a problem to be solved. This generosity shows up in the community's willingness to pay the economic and emotional prices required by creating something new. Change always brings with it the potential to hurt, and it always hurts some more than others. For churches, living into the reign of God and engendering hope in our children and youth may require community members to give up some of their entitlements or some of their power. It may require church members to put themselves into situations that are uncomfortable for them. It may mean that a church needs to stop doing some things it has done for a very long time and take risks with some incredibly new and experimental ideas. This reminds me of the words of Jesus in Matthew 10:39: "Those who find their life will lose it, and those who lose their life for my sake will find it." Episcopal priest Kerlin Richter says, "Christ calls us to die to ourselves, not remodel ourselves."[11] Your faith community may not be comfortable as it lives into God's alternative future – but it might be glorious.

One current example of this spirit of generosity in action is how churches are responding to the current movement to have children and teens more involved in corporate worship services. For much of the history of the church, children and youth always attended the worship service, but sometime in the 20th century all this changed. Churches started to hold Sunday school at the same time as the worship service or created elaborate, entertaining "children's church" programs. However, current research is showing that the non-involvement of children and youth in a church's corporate worship is detrimental to their spiritual health, as well as to the health of the broader faith community. So, many churches are exploring how to welcome children back into their worship in meaningful ways by transforming adult-centric worship practices in order to more fully extend generosity to children and youth, and to become changed by the gifts they bring.

In some churches these attempts to welcome children and youth into worship have been met with opposition from both parents and regular adult attenders of worship. Both groups demonstrate privilege and entitlement in their resistance to changes made in order to become a community of generosity. Some parents complain that they "get" nothing out of the worship service if their children are present, and other adults worry about noise and the "dumbing down" of the worship service. I saw these individualistic, consumer-based assumptions in action when one woman in a church I served remarked to me that she didn't want to see any changes to "her" worship. The attitude of entitlement stands in the way of these churches becoming transformative communities for all. Perhaps a way forward for churches that desire to be transformative communities of possibility would be to work toward a future in which they create worship that is meaningful across the generations, worship that might take people out of their comfort zones at times in order to become a space that is open to all. This might be the future they could create together.

Communities of Dissent

Fourth, communities that transform their members and the world welcome authentic dissent. Hospitality means not only welcoming the stranger, but also welcoming the strange ideas and practices she brings with her. Creating space for dissent is a way to value diversity and show respect for a wide range of beliefs. Sometimes we shut down dissent because it threatens our plans or even our strongly-held beliefs. But transformative communities tamp down the feelings of being threatened and are curious about why the dissent matters to either side. The more we disagree with the dissent, the more curious we should be about it. Such curiosity can produce alignment within what is being created even in the face of disagreement. Transformative communities model "loving our enemies" as a way of living into the alternative future. Our enemies are no longer the "theys," but are part of a greater, wider, more diverse "us."[12]

Communities that Fear Not

Fifth, transformative communities of possibility work hard to stare down anxiety. Hope in an alternative future, and anxiety about it cannot exist together. Churches can be anxious places these days, and giving in to anxiety causes them to desire a predictable future, one based on what is known and what has been rather than what is unknown and what might yet be. But a predictable future, according to Block, is not an alternative future; it is simply the future we already have, made a little better. Churches must remember that the angels told the shepherds to "fear not." We who seek to make churches into transformative communities of possibility must tell our communities to "fear not." Anxious places are not healthy places. Our children and youth need to know we believe the Jesus who said:

> Consider the lilies, how they grow: they neither toil nor spin; yet I tell
> you, even Solomon in all his glory was not clothed like one of these.
> But if God so clothes the grass of the field, which is alive today and

tomorrow is thrown into the oven, how much more will he clothe you –
you of little faith! And do not keep striving for what you are to eat
and what you are to drink, and do not keep worrying. For it is the
nations of the world that strive after all these things, and your Father
knows that you need them. Instead, strive for his kingdom, and these
things will be given to you as well (Lk 12:27-31).

Living into those words of Jesus means facing down anxiety and living into the alternative future of the reign of God. Modelling this for our children and youth will capture their imaginations as they join with us in saying no to fear and yes to an uncertain, unpredictable future.

Communities that Question

Last, a transformative community of possibility creates and lives into an alternative future by asking questions that create the space for something new to emerge. We in the church need to ask questions such as these suggested by Block:

- *What commitment do you bring to this thing we are creating together?*
- *What is the story you keep telling about the problems of this community?*
- *What is your contribution to the thing you complain about?*
- *What gifts do you hold that can be brought to bear on this new thing we are creating?*[13]

These sorts of questions help to answer the ultimate question: "What will we create together?"

According to Block, powerful questions have three qualities. First, they are ambiguous. They allow each person to bring their own context and meaning to the question. Powerful questions are not asked in a way that leads one down a particular path, but rather in a way that elicits genuine concerns, ideas, and creativity. Second, they are personal. These questions don't allow people to pass answers off onto "they" or "them." They require personal ownership, responsibility, and account-ability in their answers. For example, one might ask, "How valuable an experience do you plan to have?" And, last, the questions must awaken anxiety – but an anxiety that differs from the fearful anxiety of stuck communities.[14] This kind of anxiety makes people uncomfortable and evokes dissonance in their thinking. Nothing ever changes unless dis-equilibrium is brought to the status quo.

Engendering Hope

So what does this all mean for those of us who are immersed in faith communities and charged with faithfully forming children, youth, and adults into people who live spiritually-transformed lives? It means we need to be able to imagine, and hope for, the alterna-tive future we want to create. Jesus gave us the blueprint for the reign of God. Can we imagine a world where no one is harmed by violence? Maybe not, but Jesus could. Can we imagine a world where everyone always has enough to eat? Maybe not, but Jesus could. Can we imagine a world where love – not fear – wins? Maybe not, but Jesus could.

We have the picture. We have the possibilities in front of us. Now we just need to figure out how our faith communities will live into the charge to change the nature of our world and transform our culture as we now know it. Remember, this is not problem-solving. Problem-solv-ing can make tomorrow a little better, but in the end it still gives us the same future. The only way to create an alternative future is to change the nature of things. We have all we need through God's spirit and the stories of Jesus in order to create and live into God's picture of an alter-native future. Perhaps this is what the apostle Paul was talking about in 2 Corinthians 5:17: "So if anyone is in Christ, there is a new creation: everything old has passed away; see, everything has become new!"

The ways in which our children, youth, and adults are spiritually formed are a result of the kinds of faith communities that we have. Transformative communities are hopeful, generous, welcoming, ac-countable places where a different future – God's future – for our world is seen as something that can actually happen when we work to model and live into the reign of God within our churches. These communities will form children, youth, and adults into hopeful, generous, and welcoming people.

But actively living into the hope of God's future and the transformation it brings is not without risk. The predictable may not be satisfying but it may be quite comfortable. And the numbness of despair that helps us close our eyes to the painful events of the present and the painful lives of others in our world might even be welcome. Being prescribed active and risky hope in God's promises in place of certain comfort and temporary pain relief can seem foolish and imprudent to those around us.

But Jesus does prescribe active and risky hope amidst a despairing world. Holding on to hope in the just work of a transcendent God, working in concert with God's Spirit to bring about this new future, and passing that hope on to those around us are ways to live in the way of Jesus and create a better future together. And living in the way of Jesus is the only way we'll truly transform ourselves and our children into the sort of people Jesus calls us to be. But getting unstuck, giving up personal entitlement, accepting responsibility for the present situation, and aligning with other perspectives are the work in front of every faith community that wants to transform itself and our world. This takes courage, and this takes hope. Our children and youth will watch as we do this work, and their imaginations will be captured by a God who loves all, and by Jesus who welcomed all and healed the vicious wounds of our bent world.

Five years ago, I ended my chapter in the first volume in the *Faith Forward* series with words from philosopher Pierre Teilhard de Chardin. Since that time, our world has undergone many changes, and the seemingly insurmountable challenges that we now face make it more necessary than ever to heed those powerful words. And so I will leave you again with: "The future belongs to those who give the next generation reason for hope."

1. Peter Block, *Community: The Structure of Belonging* (San Francisco: Berrett-Koehler, 2008), 48.
2. Ibid., 37.
3. Ibid., 37.
4. Ibid., 43.
5. Ibid., 48.
6. Ibid., 105.
7. Ibid., 114.
8. Ibid., 48.
9. Ibid., 70.
10. Ibid., 127-8.
11. Quoted in "On Giving Testimony: Why 'Why Christian?' Worked", Rachel Held Evans blog, October 6, 2015. https://rachelheidevans.com/biog/why-christian-conference-recap.
12. Block, *Community*, 130ff.
13. Ibid., 106-7.
14. Ibid., 106.

10.

Stirring the Pot

Toward a Theology of Interfaith Cooperation

EBOO PATEL

Eboo Patel is a leading voice in the movement for interfaith coopera- tion, and the Founder and President of Interfaith Youth Core. He holds a doctorate from Oxford University and served on President Obama's Inaugural Faith Council. He is a regular contributor to the public conversation around religion and religious pluralism in America.

There's a well-known folk story called "Stone Soup," about how a wandering traveller brings together a village around a pot of soup to which all have contributed. It seems to me that this tale can be re-imagined as a story of interfaith leadership.

It's the story of a village where the inhabitants are starving. Imagine these inhabitants isolated in their homes, huddled together in small units, afraid of each other, afraid of their neighbours because of differences – because of diversity. They're afraid because the neighbours across the street use a different name for God, because the folks around the corner speak a different language at home, because the people around the way don't have the same food customs as they do. Their fear causes them to sit alone in their homes and avoid talking to one another. They are not sharing, and they are certainly not cooperating.

One day, a traveller rolls up into the village. She comes into the centre of the town, builds a roaring fire, and takes out of the pack on her back a large pot and a ladle. She goes down to the river and puts clean water in the pot, places the pot on the fire, and begins to stir. Although the people are inside their huts and homes with shutters closed and blinds drawn – afraid – they notice what this traveller is doing and begin to get a little curious. The children start to peek out of the windows and open the doors; they want to see what is going on. Slowly but surely, a couple of kids escape their huts and their homes and make their way down to the centre of town, where they find this fire and this pot and this woman. Bit by bit the entire village gathers, and one of the curious children says, "What are you doing?"

The woman looks up from stirring and says, "I'm making stone soup." She very conspicuously puts an enormous stone into the pot.

Hearing that she's cooking a meal, one villager explains, "Well, that's great, because we're starving. Is it done?" The traveller continues to stir, and she takes a little sip and says, "It's almost there, but it needs some potatoes." Another person says, "We've got potatoes!" and runs back to her home, fiddles in the cupboard, finds the potatoes, and brings them to the centre of town. The travelling woman chops the potatoes, throws them into the pot, and keeps on stirring.

Another child asks, "Well, is it done? We're starving!" The woman takes a little sip and says, "It's almost there, but it needs some carrots". Right away someone jumps up, exclaims, "I think we've got carrots." then runs back to his home, opens the fridge, and sees that the only thing in the fridge is carrots. He can't make a meal out of carrots alone, but he can bring them to the centre of town, chop them up, throw them into the pot – where someone else who only had potatoes has already thrown their potatoes into the pot – and stir.

And so the evening went. "Almost done. Who's got spices? Almost done. We need some zucchini."

At the end of the night, the people in this village – who, just six hours ago were starving and huddled isolated in their homes, alone, afraid of one another – were feasting. The woman watched what she had done, smiled, went back to the river, cleaned her pot, and put it in her pack. She placed the pack on her back and went on to the next village where the inhabitants were afraid of one another and starving, even though they each had ingredients that together would make a feast.

This is a story of diversity and a story of leadership. As much as we might hear rhetoric about unity in diversity, the truth is that diversity does not always bring people together. Diversity is not just about the differences we like and find interesting. And it's not just about the identities for which we immediately feel an affinity. Diversity is also about the differences and identities and allegiances that might make us uncomfortable. And so it can divide people. Diversity can erode civic community and make identity harder to pass on, more difficult to transfer. To better understand this, let me lead you into the geeky territory of social theory.

The Challenges of Diversity

In the late 1970s, sociologist Peter Berger wrote the book *The Heretical Imperative*, in which he wrote two words that changed the course of social theory: "modernity pluralizes."[1] Berger points out that what distinguishes our era from how most people have experienced life in preceding eras is that we constantly meet people who are different from us. Diversity certainly existed in human cultures and contexts before our era, but now we experience and encounter greater levels of diversity at greater frequency. Modernity pluralizes as developments in communications, technology, air travel, and cities allow us to interact in unprecedented ways with people unlike ourselves. What this means is that, while our great-grandparents largely lived in physical or psychological bubbles of homogeneity – contexts in which people across the street and people next door did the same things that they did – we who are alive today live very different lives. And while my children's elementary school is full of posters that read "multiculturalism is beautiful" and "diversity is our strength," Berger notes that although there are many positive dimensions to it, it is useful to have a clear-eyed look at the world and recognize the challenges of diversity.

The first challenge of diversity, according to Berger, is that identity moves from fate to choice.[2] My grandparents went to Jamatkhana, the Ismaili Muslim house of worship, because their parents went to Jamatkhana, and everyone in their physical and psychological bubble went to Jamatkhana. Identity was fate. Friday nights were for Jamatkhana. God created Friday nights for this purpose. We would wake up and pray Dua, and before bed we would pray Dua, and this was how the world was.

But when people move in next door and don't go to Jamatkhana on Friday nights, and don't pray Dua in the morning and at night, all of a sudden the experience of one's identity isn't fate anymore. All at once the presence of an alternative makes us think to ourselves, "Why do I do what I do?" Passing on a tradition now becomes much more difficult.

Berger goes one step further into the territory many of us live in: religious communities.[3] He says religious communities were at one time places that were taken for granted. Their status was taken for granted. In other words, church was just what Sunday mornings were for. But now religious communities are voluntary associations. Now you must prove to people that what you do on Sunday mornings at 10 a.m. is more interesting than the thousand other alternatives. This makes it much more difficult to pass on a tradition. The inhabitants of the starving village had reasons to be afraid of one another. Parents had expectations of how their children were to speak, and they taught this in their homes. But if they were to send their children to a different home, where children talk to their parents in a different way, will the visiting kids come back home and talk to their parents differently?

I have two children, eight and 11 years old, and before they were born, this concept was abstract to me. It is not abstract anymore. I have expectations for how my children will talk to me, but the children down the way may not talk to their parents that way. That's called diversity. I have the expectation that my children will pray before bedtime. "But Dad," they'll say, "when the babysitter comes over, she doesn't make us do that." That's called diversity. Diversity makes it more difficult to pass on a tradition. It interrupts identity continuity.

The second challenge, according to Berger, is that diversity makes civic community more difficult. Robert Putnam, in his study "*E Pluribus Unum*," examines trends in ethnic diversity and civic community, of which the latter is measured by voting rates, volunteerism, reported trust rates, and the number of people who say they know their neighbours.[4] Putnam found that the more diverse a community becomes, the lower the rate of trust is. The lower the rate of volunteerism. The lower the rate of voting. Unhappy with these findings, Putnam turns and twists and mangles his data every way he can think of and continues to get the same result. Diversity erodes community. He's speaking not of identity community, as in Christian, Muslim, or Jewish community, but civic community, as in northside of Chicago, Cambridge, Massachusetts, or Seattle, Washington.

Bridges Don't Fall from the Sky

With these challenges in mind, we can see why the stone soup story becomes an important example. The trends associated with both challenges can be reversed – it just takes a little work!

It takes the right kind of leadership. And when we consider leadership, the most common metaphor for what I want to do with diversity is "build bridges." My best idea in 15 years is that bridges do not fall from the sky or rise from the ground; they are built by people. The starving inhabitants of the village had all the ingredients within the village to make a feast. It just required a leader who had three things: a vision, a knowledge base, and the necessary set of skills.

First, a leader needs a vision. She needs the ability to see a group of disparate people, a random assortment of people who happen to occupy the same geographical space, as a community. This is vision; it is a unique way of seeing. Marcel Proust, the great French writer, says the true journey of discovery is not going to new landscapes; it is in developing new eyes.[5] Pastors and active laypeople do this every Sunday. They enter their church and, rather than seeing 200 random people, they see that they can collectively will each other into a community. That is a vision. That is a unique way of seeing the world. In the stone soup story, the traveller enters the village and says, "You don't just occupy the same three square miles; you are a community."

Second, a leader needs a knowledge base. I know that the Muslim family in their home brings to the table a religious and civilizational heritage that lifts up the value of mercy. For the purposes of the stone soup story, let's concretize that as potatoes. I know that the Jewish family in their home, because of their religious and civilizational heritage, brings with them the contribution of *tikkun olam*, repairing the world. Let's concretize that as carrots. In other words, part of what a leader does in a diverse setting is to recognize and know the different contributions that members of the community can offer, such as the civilizational and religious parts of the identity traditions that people bring to a diverse area. This is the reason I love Obama's inaugural speech, in which he said, "Our patchwork heritage is a strength, not a weakness. We are a nation of Christians and Muslims, Jews and Hindus, and non-believers. We are shaped by every language and culture, drawn from every end of this Earth." The United States, along with so many other places on this planet, is a nation to which many kinds of people have contributed. Leaders need a knowledge base so they can truly recognize the potential contributions of all members of a diverse community; so that what they know about Islam, for example, isn't just what's on the first minute of the evening news.

Finally, a leader must possess skills. In the stone soup story, the traveller had the skills to create an activity in which people wanted to participate by cooperating and sharing. Many times, those of us with a vision and a knowledge base think that if we shout our vision and our knowledge loudly enough, stone soup will automatically happen. It would be as if the traveller rolled up into the village and shouted, "Hey you fools, bring your carrots and your potatoes and you can feed each other."

People who work with children know that this sort of strategy doesn't work. We cannot harangue 11-year-olds. No matter how beautiful and crystal clear the truth is, we are not going to lecture 11-year-olds into believing it. We must create activities for them to take part in.

The brilliance of the traveller in the stone soup story is that she knew that stirring a stone in a pot over a fire in the centre of town would evoke people's curiosity. She knew that they would come and ask what she was doing, giving her the opportunity to say something enticing, such as, "I'm making something to feed you, a starving village." She knew that somebody would likely then ask if it were done, and she would get to say that it needed this one ingredient, and that a group in the village likely had it. And then that group over there likely had the second ingredient. And the group over there likely had the third.

In order to create community for people with diverse identities, world views, and backgrounds, an effective leader needs a vision, a knowledge base, and a skill set. A leader cannot create community without these three essential ingredients, and without community, the people share only a geographical space and do not have a true sense of belonging. We often think that if we interact too frequently with the people next door who are different from us our identity continuity will be challenged. It takes a leader with a vision, a knowledge base, and a skill set, and one who can actualize these things, to weave the group together into a community. This is how bridges between diverse groups of people are built.

Who May Sing Gregorian Chant?

While there are many aspects to building bridges amidst diversity, my focus has been on those erected among faith communities and religious traditions. And so I read within the stone soup story a specific dimension having to do with the importance of the theology of interfaith cooperation. When we speak of interfaith cooperation, we need to remember that there are two things that we are collectively attempting to do.

First, it is part of my value-system – and likely yours as well – to continue an identity tradition. I want my kids to be Muslim. This matters to me. It is that simple. I don't want them to be the kind of Muslim who erects barriers to their Christian or Jewish or atheist neighbours, nor the kind of Muslim who hides away in isolation. And certainly not the kind of Muslim who uses bludgeons to dominate others. I want them to be the kind of Muslim who builds bridges out of the stones of the Islamic heritage. If you're reading this book, my guess is that you want your children to be Christian. You want them to be part of continuing this 2,000-year-old tradition called Christianity. And so we have this desire to continue our identity tradition in common.

Second, I care about civic community. I live in this place called the United States of America. Some scholars say it is the most religiously diverse country in human history.[6] It has people from more religious communities, sects, traditions, and offshoots, and more diverse groups of people, than any other political entity at any other time in human history. All of us who live in this country have a collective stake in this reality. We want our civic community to be strong and resilient and beautiful. And the same goes for so many other countries, which are also experiencing unprecedented levels of diversity.

So, we want both things for our children: we want them to be Christian, or Muslim, or Jewish, or Hindu, and we want a strong, collective community called Chicago, or the United States, or the world. Connecting these two desires can be a tremendous challenge.

The answer to this challenge is a theology of interfaith cooperation. Such a theology connects our identities and desires as people of faith to those we possess as members of a shared civic community. Part of who one is as a Christian involves contributing as a good neighbour to the collective, diverse civic society in which one lives, whether in the United Kingdom, Australia, India, or my home, the United States. Part of the reason one does this is because building a common good in which Christians can thrive means Muslims and Jews and others can thrive in it also. There may be underlying principles like religious freedom, but pursuing such a society is not just a civic or a constitutional value. It is a sacred value. Building a common good is part of who we are as Christians, or Muslims, or Jews. To advance this concept, we need to have a knowledge base that includes a theology of interfaith cooperation.

One of my close friends in interfaith work is a young man named Nick Price, an evangelical pastor who came through the InterVarsity system at the University of Illinois. He became a staff member at InterVarsity and is now a Missouri Synod pastor. A few years ago, he shared with me that in the Bible there is both the great commission and the great cooperation. There is a value around proselytizing and a value around cooperating. Both are sacred and ought to be executed in different ways and in different spaces. I already knew about the great commission, so I asked him to tell me about the great cooperation. "It is right there in the Good Samaritan story," he said as he opened his Bible so we could read through the story. Nick related to me that this is an interfaith story.

I have been teaching in Christian seminaries for many years, and I'd say that about half of the students I've worked with would say the Good Samaritan was their favorite story. Whenever I would ask them why they love this story, they would say to me, as the good, progressive Christians that they were, that it lifts up the value of the "other." But I had never really known what kind of "other" this Samaritan was.

To help me better understand, Nick flipped to the story of the woman at the well in John 4, and asked me to read it. He helped me see that what Jesus was doing in this repartee with the woman at the well was engaging in doctrinal dispute. He is telling her that she prays to a God she does not know, that she prays at the wrong temple.

Nick then asked me, "Who are the Samaritans?" I realized that they were not just some random other but that they were, specifically, a *theological* other. They were the religious others – the Muslims, the Jains, or the Hindus. In this light, the Good Samaritan story takes on a whole new cast, because we can better understand what Jesus said in response to the question about how a person gains eternal life. Jesus told the man who asked this question not to follow the ethic of the leaders of his religious community – the priest and the Levite – but instead to follow the ethic of the Samaritan, the very individual with whom he has doctoral disagreements. "Go and do likewise."

This evangelical Missouri Synod Lutheran pastor believes he must take this story seriously. Evangelicals are supposed to have a high view of scripture. Deep in the bones of the tradition, at the very root of this faith, is this story of when the ethic of the religious other – the person with whom you have doctrinal disputes – is superior; a story of when nothing less than salvation is on the line. Go and do likewise.

This is a theology of interfaith cooperation. It is here in scripture that Christians are commanded by the tradition to engage in partnerships with people from other religions, not to win them to their faith through the great commission, but to work in partnership with them according to the great cooperation. Dietrich Bonhoeffer, the great German Lutheran pastor, upon seeing the destruction of Jewish neighbourhoods by Nazis one night went on German radio the next day and said, "Only those who cry out for the Jews may sing Gregorian chant."[7] He wasn't making this up; it is biblical. To be in partnership with the religious other is not just a nice thing to do, or a neighbourly thing to do; it is a Christian thing to do. It's right there in scripture.

Prophets, Birds, and the Presence of the Sacred

The holy month of Ramadan is a month of fasting and purification for Muslims. The fasting is not just a ritual practice; it is also connected to perhaps the most important moment in history for Muslims – the first revelations. In the year 610, a merchant named Muhammad from the city of Mecca made his annual pilgrimage during the month of Ramadan to a cave on Mount Hira. As he had done for many years, Muhammad fasted and prayed. But on one of the odd nights in the last ten days of Ramadan, which we call *Laylat al-Qadr* (the Night of Power), Muslims believe that Muhammad felt himself gripped by this enveloping force. The force spoke the word *Iqraa* to him, which means "recite," and Muhammad replied that he wasn't a reciter, meaning that he was not one of the poets in pagan Mecca known as reciters. The force squeezed him a second time, even tighter than the last. "*Iqraa*," it spoke. And Muhammad again said that he was not a reciter. The third time the force virtually squeezed the life out of him, again saying *"Iqraa."* But this time the first words chronologically of the Qur'an came pouring from Muhammad's mouth: "Recite in the name of your Lord who created humankind from a clot of blood."

Some traditions say that Muhammad was so afraid that he didn't know what had happened to him, and he thought he was possibly possessed by a demon, by jinn. So he went to the person he loved and trusted above all others, his wife, Khadijah, and he related the story. Khadijah said that she didn't know what had happened either, but she was sure that God had not forsaken her husband. "I am sure that God has not allowed you to be possessed by jinn," she said to Muhammad. "You are too pious and good a man." Khadijah then said that her uncle Waraqa, who was learned in the scriptures, would know what had happened. Khadijah took her husband to Waraqa, a man wrapped in his robes (at least that's how I imagine him) and told him the story. As Muhammad shivered, still shaken from what had happened, Waraqa looked in his eyes and kissed him on the forehead, saying, "Verily, the prophet of your people has arrived."

Who is Waraqa? What does it mean to be learned in the scriptures in the early seventh century in the western half of the Arabian Peninsula? These scriptures were the texts of the Christian Bible. Waraqa was a Christian monk who never converted to Islam and, as the sources suggest, Muhammad never asked him to convert. This means that the first person to recognize the prophethood of Muhammad and what many people view as a competing religious civilization was a Christian. As a theology of interfaith cooperation is inextricably woven throughout the biblical tradition, so too is it woven into the Muslim tradition. I tell my children this.

Of course, this does not make interfaith cooperation easy. It does not make diversity easy. But it makes it a requirement – a theological requirement. To be Muslim means to be in positive relationship with the diversity around you, with even the identities that you disagree with, and with even the differences you don't like. There are ways to be in positive relationship with this sort of diversity. It is a theological requirement to find and practice these ways. To do so is to advance the continuity of our identity communities – Muslim, Christian, and so forth. It makes it more likely that our children will be Christian or Muslim, and we should not feel bad for wanting them to be part of our communities of identity, because it is important. It is important to me that my children take part in building a civic community amongst people who don't view the Bible as the core sacred text and who do not pray to God in Arabic. This is a theology of interfaith cooperation.

Nine hundred years ago, Farid ud-Din Attar wrote a children's story in the Islamic tradition called "The Conference of the Birds." Attar writes that the birds are bereft, forlorn, and sad because of all the species of animals, theirs does not have a king. One of the birds, the hoopoe bird, comes forward and says, "We do have a king, and it is called the great Simorgh. We must travel a long distance to see this king, and I will bring you." Attar describes the challenge of this great journey to the Simorgh. These birds who wanted a king only five minutes ago are now complaining about the journey. "We would rather just stay in our home, huddled up, isolated, and complain about the world," they say.

The hoopoe must act as an interfaith leader. The hoopoe must be like the traveller from the stone soup story. It must figure out a way of talking to the various birds – the falcon, the eagle, and the hawk – and tell each bird how the journey is going to be good for each one of them. The hoopoe needs to find a way to make the journey appeal to the needs and lives of each bird; the hoopoe needs to have a knowledge base of the nuances of each of these birds alongside the vision to travel to the great Simorgh.

The hoopoe finally weaves together a crew of birds and skillfully leads them through seven valleys and seven challenges. The birds arrive at the gates, behind which hides the great Simorgh. Every one of them is excited. There are 30 birds left after this arduous journey, and they cannot wait to see their king. The gates open and a shimmering lake lies before them, pure as a polished mirror. In the lake, they see a reflection of themselves. You see, in Persian, *Simorgh* means 30 birds (*si* means 30, *morgh* means birds).

The story that Attar tells shows that when a group from any particular species chooses to take a journey together and is led by somebody who has the vision that such a disparate crew could call themselves a community, the knowledge of how to talk to each one in its nuanced way, and the skills to create an activity in which they all want to participate, when the journey is completed it becomes sacred. It is like seeing your king. It is like what Hindus call darshan, a witnessing of the godhead. That pathway, that process, that journey, that theology of interfaith cooperation is a holy thing. A diverse group of people becoming a community is nothing short of sacred. In the presence of such holiness, in the words of the great Chicagoan poet Gwendolyn Brooks, we can realize that "we are each other's harvest. We are each other's business. We are each other's magnitude and bond."

1. Peter Berger, *The Heretical Imperative: Contemporary Possibilities of Religious Affirmation*. (Garden City, NY: Anchor Press/ Doubleday, 1979).
2. Peter Berger, *The Many Altars of Modernity: Toward a Paradigm for Religion in a Pluralist Age* (Boston: De Gruyter, 2014).
3. Ibid.
4. Robert D. Putnam, "*E Pluribus Unum*: Diversity and Community in the Twenty-first Century," Scandinavian Political Studies 30, no. 2 (2007): 137-74.
5. Marcel Proust, *In Search of Lost Time, Vol. 1: The Way by Swann's*, trans. by Lydia Davis (New York: Penguin, 2000).
6. See Diana L. Eck, *A New Religious America: How a "Christian Country" Has Become the World's Most Religiously Diverse Nation* (San Francisco: HarperSanFrancisco, 2002).
7. See Ferdinand Schlingensiepen, *Dietrich Bonhoeffer, 1906-1945: Martyr, Thinker, Man of Resistance* (London: T&T Clark, 2010), 300.

11.

Gospel Remix

OTIS MOSS III

Rev. Dr. Otis Moss III
is Senior Pastor of
Trinity United Church
of Christ in Chicago
and author of
*Redemption in a Red
Light District, The
Gospel Re-Mix*, and
*Blue Note Preaching in
a Post-Soul World*. A
highly-regarded
preacher, Rev. Dr.
Moss is an ordained
minister in the
Progressive National
Baptist Convention
and the United
Church of Christ.

Isn't it fascinating how films have a tendency to speak theologically around certain issues? In 1999 an incredibly talented and amazing brother from Philadelphia by the name of M. Night Shyamalan wrote and directed a film entitled *The Sixth Sense*. The lead actor was Bruce Willis, and this was probably one of his best films. *The Sixth Sense*, for those of you who might not have seen this film, is about a boy who may have either extrasensory perception or severe psychological issues. And he delivers a particular line several times over the course of the movie: "I see dead people, but they don't know it yet."

It seems this sentiment could also apply when it comes to the church. In the production called life, there could very well be someone – perhaps a person who has extrasensory perception or severe psychological issues – looking at the church and saying, "I see dead churches, but they don't know it yet."

If previous church-going generations are to connect with the current generation, there must be some recognition of the major changes that have happened within our culture. The church must recognize that we are truly in a "post-Christian age." This means, in part, that the church community and the church steeple no longer hold the same meaning for younger generations. Diana Butler Bass, an historian who writes about religion and culture in the United States, tells a story about a picture in her home. The picture is of a beautiful vista and a waterfall, and she says that when she looks at it, she feels great peace. But every time she walks past the picture, she also thinks that she needs to change the frame. Because something is wrong with the frame, and the inappropriate frame changes the way she looks at the picture.

The same goes for our faith. Christianity is a beautiful picture, one that can bring tremendous peace. But, in many ways it has the wrong frame. A shift must be made in terms of how faith is framed so that the picture of Christianity can be seen in different and radical ways. Changing the frame can shift the way we see the world – and ourselves.

The Barna Group, a Christian-based polling firm, facilitated a study in early 2017 that identified a growing segment of the population who "love Jesus but not the church."[1] Interestingly, the folks behind this study interviewed millennials and found that there was a major disconnect between Jesus and the church. According to the study, when millennials were asked about Jesus, they replied with words such as *That's my man. I like Jesus. Jesus is alright with me. He's about compassion, he's about love, he's about justice. I'm down with Jesus. I love Jesus. He's alright.* But when asked the same question about the church, their answers were completely different. They said that the church is judgmental, racist, and homophobic, has a doctrine that doesn't make sense, and is problematic overall.

Do we see the problem? Part of the challenge is that the church has not yet recognized that older generations frame faith in ways that are alien to newer generations. More and more, young people are living in a post-soul age, or a post-Christian age, as opposed to a postmodern age.

Tracing the Post-Soul Age

But what exactly is a post-soul age? In order to define this, we need to examine what a "soul age" is, and it may be helpful to do this through the lens of African-American culture. Many African Americans grew up in a soul age, or knew someone who came out of the soul era.

Once upon a time, almost any African-American artist who sang or played what was considered to be popular music came out of a particular faith narrative or faith tradition. That artist or musician usually took that which they learned within that particular faith tradition and spread it out on to a stage before the entire world. Before Aretha Franklin could sing anything about R-E-S-P-E-C-T, she had to sing in her father's church. Before Marvin Gaye said anything about "What's Going On," he was in a Pentecostal church where his father was the pastor. Before Jackie Wilson could sing, or before any particular artist who is considered to be a soul artist could perform, they had history with a particular narrative of faith. Soul music came out of the church. A soul age is one in which young people were embedded in a community of faith.

As history and music moved forward, we arrived at hip hop culture. Hip hop culture is the first African-American creation, or contribution to a broader American culture, that does not directly come out of a faith narrative. Spirituals and gospel music, the blues, jazz, and R&B are all connected to the church, however you want to define "the church." But hip hop is the first cultural creation that stands just outside the window of the church, looking in. So many young people were "put out" of the church, some literally and others figuratively, because the church was arguing about things that had nothing to do with their existential experience. The church wasn't talking about the things that the young people were dealing with day to day.

Hip hop culture is not a new creation. It began in the South Bronx in 1972 with DJ Kool Herc, a creative young man with West Indian roots. The story goes that he loved music and was heavily influenced by his father's large collection of James Brown records. Herc didn't have enough money to buy a drum set or a guitar, so he used two turntables and a microphone to create sounds. These sounds were crafted by taking two albums and mixing the audio together while the music played. This technique is now commonly known as "mixing and scratching."

Herc used his creativity, fuelled by poverty and necessity, to create something new. He then took his new technology and said, "I want to make some money off of it since people enjoy what I'm doing. Instead of just spinning records, I'm going to do something unique." And so, from 1972 to 1979, it was the DJ – the disc jockey – who was the premier artist in certain urban areas. There was no such thing as rap music at that time. The only reasons for a voice to ring through the speakers were the DJ's interplay with the audience, or the DJ's need for a bathroom break.

As it happened, the persons providing verbal entertainment during the interlude were just as creative as the main attraction, and the lyricist soon began to take the spotlight. The person who took the stage when the DJ went to the bathroom suddenly moved out front and became the featured performer. Young people between the ages of 12 and 18 in New York, largely in the South Bronx, Brooklyn, Queens, and Staten Island, began to use their lyrical creativity to rhyme about the greatness of their neighbourhoods, their friends, and themselves. But most people in the United States never even heard the music until 1979.

In that year a song came out by a group that was based in Harlem, New York, in a place called Sugar Hill – the same place where W. E. B. Du Bois and Ida Wells worked during the Harlem Renaissance. The group called itself the Sugar Hill Gang, and the song was "Rapper's Delight." Their record went national in a hurry, and even though it was a sound that was not then commonplace, it was quickly taken up by the mainstream.

A few years later, another shift occurred through the work of a gentleman by the name of Grandmaster Flash, as well as his Furious Five. In 1982, this group used their creativity to do something that the church was not doing: they critiqued poverty and racism. They entitled their anthem "The Message."

> *Don't push me 'cause I'm close to the edge*
> *I'm trying not to lose my head*
> *It's like a jungle sometimes*
> *It makes me wonder how I keep from goin' under*[2]

"The Message" raised Black collective consciousness during the middle years of the Reagan administration, when youth unemployment was 70 percent. God will send prophets when prophets in the church refuse to preach.

During the 1980s, community riots had to take on a prophetic role because the church was involved in other concerns, such as adding a contemporary service or using drums during worship. These and other things did not resonate with many in the neighbourhoods adjacent to the buildings in which these "worship wars" were fought. While the church argued with itself, an entire group decided that those issues had nothing to do with their day-to-day reality. "We're going to hell in a hand basket," they exclaimed. So they took it upon themselves to critique poverty and racism.

A Nightmare Wrapped in a Dream

That decision birthed a consciousness that lived outside of the church walls. One of the drawbacks to this "new" consciousness, however, was corporate commodification. It is important to point out that it was at this point in United States' history that Federal Communications Commission (FCC) rules were loosened so that a person, or entity, could not only own a radio station, but also a record company, a television station, and a newspaper. Those with money who owned these media outlets saw there was money to be made in this new music. But there was a problem. Those media moguls with money collectively said to Black artists, "You know what? We like this music, but the consciousness is problematic. You're talking too much about racism. You're talking too much about poverty. We don't like that, because we are not selling to Black children; we are selling to White suburban youth. And we want you to talk about pathology that we are comfortable with, that we have already framed as a stereotype for people who've been kissed by nature's sun. So, we would prefer you to speak about the problems instead of critiquing the system."

Thus the commodification of Black consciousness began in the music industry. Corporations sold young people, especially those in high school, a nightmare wrapped in a dream. An offer of something like a three-year deal for $35,000 a year might have seemed like all the money in the world to a 16-year-old artist, but in reality it was barely a drop in the proverbial bucket. Community consciousness was hijacked by the media moguls with money and pimped into something called "gangsta rap," which had also been hatched in Black communities and on Black street corners, but was ultimately evangelized in the corporate boardroom. And the media moguls with money found success with their project because 70 percent of hip hop music is purchased by white suburban youth, who would rather hear a Black artist talk about issues within their community than critique the system that creates those issues. Put more plainly, this approach is the equivalent of talking about saving babies that keep drowning in a river, rather than going up river to find out why people are throwing babies into the river in the first place. This beautiful, amazing, incredible music called hip hop has been taken over by corporate media, and babies keep drowning in the river.

An 8-Track Church in a Streaming World

Meanwhile, the church was doing what the church has always done: closing her eyes to new opportunity. And while her eyes were closed she confused method and message.

Sticking with the music theme, let's think about the church like this. The song "Amazing Grace" needs to be played during a particular worship experience. The church is equipped with an 8-track player, but the person responsible for bringing the music wants to stream the song from the Internet. The church's response to the request to play the song using a different technology is something along the lines of, "We only use 8-track cassettes here. That is how it has always been." Those attending the worship experience never get to hear the song because the new method of delivery was discredited.

The church is an 8-track church in a streaming world. The main reason the church can't connect with this generation of youth is because it is so caught up in deifying a methodology that it rejects the message.

But Jesus never does anything the same way twice. For some people, all Jesus needs to do is let them touch the hem of his garment and everything is all right. For somebody else, Jesus spits on the ground, scoops up some mud, and slaps it on their eyes. For somebody else, Jesus just says, "Go on home, everything's going to be okay." Jesus always uses a methodology that reflects the context; his words and actions change in order to reflect what is going on in a particular time and place and with particular people. It would be oppressive for Jesus to say, "Because I healed this person in this way, I must do the same with you, even though your context is different."

The woman with the issue of blood is a great example here.[3] She's a real sister on a major level. Jesus is on his way to heal a 12-year-old girl when he encounters the woman. This woman is one of the few people in the Bible who basically says, "I'm taking my healing." As Jesus is walking along, minding his own business, she reaches out to touch the hem of his garment. She says to herself, "I know that if I just touch the hem of his garment, everything's going to…" Isn't that something? That's a bad sister! She says, "I don't care who's in my way, I'm going to get what I need."

This brings to mind a second sister in the Bible, the one who argues Jesus into healing her daughter.[4] Jesus says, "I'm sorry, I cannot provide for you." The woman replies, "Even the dogs eat the crumbs from the table." Jesus then heals the woman's daughter, despite his initial refusal. These two stories are perfect examples of Jesus considering the context of the person with whom he is dealing.

Unfortunately, we often seek a one-size-fits-all solution, which is not what Jesus modelled. The way things work on the south side of Chicago won't necessarily work the same way in Appleton, Wisconsin. Context matters, even though the message is the same.

The Church in a Post-Soul Age

This brings us to the incredibly important context of our young people. We have seen how we have journeyed to a post-soul age, an age in which the things that have been created in culture are not directly connected to the church. These creations might have some sort of affiliation with the church, but they are not directly connected. Now that we know where we are, so to speak, the fundamental question becomes: *What should the church do in a post-soul age?*

For one thing, we need to tell the truth. The church cannot sequester itself, unable to speak the truth about what is happening in the world. But being part of the world will bring challenges to one's faith and raise questions. And we shouldn't be afraid of this. I've long heard it said that God is not to be questioned. But maybe it's time to rethink this. After all, God can handle questions. God isn't intimidated by our questions. If Jesus questions God from a cross, then why can't everyone have honest conversations with God? Questions for and about God should be allowed to fester and to flow within a ministry. The truth must be told, and sometimes truth comes in the form of a question.

Secondly, in this post-soul age there must be a return to the Spirit. We need a level of Pentecostalism within the church. This is not about denomination. This is about a movement that is deeply connected to the African and African-American traditions, a movement of the Spirit that was started by William Seymour.[5] Seymour, who was considered to be three-fifths of a human being because he was kissed by nature's sun, did not have full intellectual capacity and could not even sit in a classroom. He had to sit outside and listen through a classroom window.[6] But he felt that God had touched him and called him to go to Los Angeles, where he occupied an empty former African Methodist Episcopal church on Azusa Street. It was there that a small group of African-American worshipers had their first service in early 1906, and it was recorded that they didn't even have a pulpit. All they had were a bunch of shoeboxes that they stacked together, and from behind which Seymour would preach. It gives a whole new meaning to God ordering your steps, when you have shoeboxes around you!

One of the most remarkable things about this move of the Spirit was the gathering together of different races and ethnicities. What started among a group of African Americans expanded to include all sorts of people. This was in the early 1900s at the height of segregation in the United States, evidenced by the Scottsboro case and lynching. But despite all of this heated and violent division, a diverse group of people – Black and White, Latino and Asian – all gathered in one space. The leadership could be classified as "ethical restorationist," which means they "abandoned the conventional means by which society ordered reality (education, social status, race, and gender categories); in doing so, they assaulted the status quo."[7] Some even say there was a group of Latino people present who couldn't speak English, and even though the Black people couldn't speak Spanish, they said the Spirit was moving and they understood each other. Yes, the Spirit was moving.

But then some people from the North showed up. They'd heard about these things that were happening on Azusa Street every night, about these barriers that were being broken, and they didn't like what they heard. It's said that during a visit from these outsiders, a woman, who happened to be White and a deacon, caught the Spirit. And in that moment she fell back into the arms of a man, who happened to be Black. At that moment, the visiting northerners decided that they had to end this movement right away. They made it their mission in life to put together propaganda to destroy this movement. And in many ways, they succeeded. They started their own denominations that said women have no role and Black people have no leadership, but they too called themselves Pentecostal. Seymour's heart was broken. Having seen the Spirit break down barriers, he was now witnessing racism position itself as a greater god to people in the United States. It is said that he died of a broken heart. He believed that the Spirit could break just about everything...but it couldn't break the racism that people worshiped in America.

What would happen if there were a genuine spiritual revival that broke down barriers? What would come about if we recognized the heart-to-heart and mind-to-mind and spirit-to-spirit within our churches? Christian activist Shane Claiborne believes there are cracks and fissures happening within the evangelical movement because people who grew up within it now recognize all the lies they have been told. Jesus was concerned about poverty and racism, about equal justice, and about literacy – not personal piety. Claiborne can see that fissures are breaking open. In other words, a Pentecostal spirit of truth-telling and justice-centred focus is happening right now.

In the Chicagoland area, Black Youth Project 100 is one of the few ministries that have people involved in Black Lives Matter. BYP 100 is a "safe space" where they know and understand that there's a deep spiritual connection to the movement that itself has a goal of shifting some of the systemic ills of our nation. We need truth-telling. And we need a movement of the Spirit. And both must be justice-centred.

Taking Hip Hop to Church

The creativity of hip hop wonderfully frames the reinvigoration of ministry. According to Tricia Rose, who chronicles the history of hip hop in *Black Noise: Rap Music and Black Culture in Contemporary America*, there are four pillars to hip hop.[8] As I see it, these pillars have a lot to offer those of us seeking to reinvigorate the church.

The first pillar Rose names is DJ-ing. The DJ is the one who understands the utilization and appropriation of technology. In the church, there are all sorts of ministries utilizing and appropriating technology. For example, the technologies of social media and social networking are being used in the church to connect people in new ways. At Trinity United Church of Christ, we have a Digi – or Digital – Pastor whose job it is to minister to people in virtual spaces. This staff member has a bigger "church" than the senior pastor because the digital church is roughly 15,000 to 20,000 people. The job of Digi Pastor is to build a network, along with cells that focus on specific issues, around the nation. The goal is not for more people to join Trinity, but for Trinity to figure out how it can make a loving impact where it's located. All of this is done with the appropriation of technology.

The second pillar is graffiti. This doesn't mean we should all go out and cover the walls of our churches with spray paint. Graffiti is more than spray paint; it's the appropriation of aesthetic space. With this in mind, it's possible to see that faith and graffiti have something in common. Graffiti can be thought of as an artist's attempt to beautify a particular space because they recognize they have "ownership" over it. The church is a space that has its fair share of graffiti; some people just call it stained glass. While the use of stained glass in churches is now formalized, it was street art before Constantine accepted Christianity. Staining glass was underground art that was elevated to church windows.

The return to the utilization of different forms of art within worship is powerful, especially for young people. At Trinity, we try to partner with a variety of other groups, one of which involves artists; we now have an artist-in-residence program. Out of this, we launched a comic book program that teaches people how to write comics. It is incredibly powerful for Black children to write comics because they get to be the hero. My family has an annual trip to Comic-Con and every year I try to find comics that feature a young girl of colour as the main character. I want my daughter to read those comics and see herself as a hero. My daughter should not define heroic activity based solely on the activities and opinions of a White 12-year-old boy. The hero can come in many forms, many colours, and from many cultures.

In Trinity's comic book program, my son created a comic book called *World War Art*, about a world where art is outlawed. In the story, misfit children of different colours and from different cultures come together. All they have are spray cans of paint in their back pockets. They go into Chicago and spray what was then the Sears Tower. In the story, the children add beautiful colour to a drab world. They are the revolutionaries. I was proud.

God is the greatest artist of all time. Every time I walk in creation, I see something that is awe-inspiring. God spends so much time on one blade of grass, or one simple snowflake. In the context of the church, we must allow for the appropriation of aesthetic space; we must add beauty into a drab and dreary world. We must allow graffiti to colour the walls.

The third pillar of hip hop is kinetics. Kinetic movement is better known as dancing, or, in the hip-hop world, break dancing. The utilization of dance is necessary because there are some things that we just can't communicate with words or pictures. There are some things that only the body can say. Unfortunately, there is a fear of the body that is taking hold in Western society. Children and adults alike are being told not to move in certain ways because of how such movement might be interpreted. But in the global South, if a person wants to effectively communicate with somebody, they need to know how to dance. They need to know how to move. Every child who comes into the world intuitively knows how to move in order to communicate. And so everybody knows at some level how to dance. We come into the world already having a beat because we've been listening to our mother's heartbeat for nine months. But we tend to squash the beat once the child is born.

The church must have dance. Some things can only be communicated by movement of the body.

The final pillar of hip hop is rapping. I'm not advocating that people need to rap in churches. But the church must let the poets be poets. All prophets are poets – and poets are prophets – because the poet says things and speaks things that no one else can or does. That is why when the psalmist David is moving in a certain direction, a poet we call a prophet by the name of Nathan has to bring him back to centre. The poet Amos speaks about justice and how it rushes down like a river and water. Jeremiah is a poet who talks about the fire shut up in his bones.

All these poets use allegory and metaphor to communicate, because when one's communicating about things that are sacred, one can only use language that says what the sacred is *like*...not what it *is*. The sacred is so expansive, so powerful, so beyond our comprehension, that it can only truly be expressed with poetry. This is why poetry is preeminent within the African-American tradition, whether spoken through music or from the pulpit. The use of poetry helps people make sense of an absurd world.

So let the poet be a prophet. Let the prophet be a poet. Let them speak in bars, spit lyrics, and use verse. Let the poet be the poet, and watch something new come out in the process.

When the church chooses not to be afraid of these four pillars, when we tell the truth, when we allow the Spirit to move and give us new experiences, and when we recognize that we have a foundation of justice in all that we do, God will create something new.

Gumbo City

One of my favourite cities is New Orleans. It's a city that has given birth to great music. It's a city full of mysticism; sacred and profane at the same time. There's something about New Orleans. It's unlike any other place in the country because it brings together everything that is uniquely American and makes something new. It is truly a gumbo.

Several years ago, my wife and I walked through the French Quarter of New Orleans and went into a studio where an artist was displaying and selling some beautiful pieces of his own creation. I was taken aback when I saw two paintings hanging very near each other that had very different price tags. One was selling for $20 and the other for $1,500. I stood there trying to figure it out: Why is one piece $1,500 and the other $20?

I finally asked the artist to explain the difference to me. He pointed to a bunch of $20 pieces and replied, "Oh, I painted those over there, but God did these over here."

"Wait a minute," I said. "Your name is on all of them. Please explain it to me. Did God just show up and just start painting for you?"

After a bit more back and forth, the artist finally told me what he had done, and what he said deeply moved my spirit. "Well, these I paint by myself. But as I was painting one time, a storm was on the horizon here in New Orleans, and God spoke to me and said, 'After you finish doing all of your work, while the paint is still wet, take your easel and place your picture out in the storm. When the storm comes, I will finish your painting.' And I said that I would take my paintings out there. And all of a sudden the rain and the wind beat against the canvases and created colours I never thought could be created. An image would come forth that was different than what I thought possible. And when I saw the beauty of that, I realized that people wanted that. That's why it's so expensive. That's a painting that God finished."

As you experiment with what ministry with children and youth looks like in the world in which we live, don't try to finish the painting by yourself. Take it out into the storm. Let God do God's work. And as God beats against the canvas of one's spirit and one's heart, something new will be created.

Let God do God's work.

1. https://www.barna.com/research/meet-love-jesus-not-church/. Dan Kimball wrote a book entitled They Like Jesus but Not the Church a decade earlier. Dan Kimball, *They Like Jesus but Not the Church: Insights from Emerging Generations* (Grand Rapids:Zondervan, 2007).
2. Grandmaster Flash and Furious Five. *The Message*. San Francisco, CA:DBK Works, 2005.
3. See Matthew 9:20–22, Mark 5:25–34, and Luke 8:43–48.
4. See Matthew 12:22-28 and Mark 7:25-30.
5. Joe Creech, "Visions of Glory: The Place of the Azusa Street Revival in Pentecostal History," *Church History: Studies in Christianity and Culture* 65, no. 3 (1996): 405-406.
6. Ibid., 412.
7. Ibid., 412.
8. See Tricia Rose, *Black Noise: Rap Music and Black Culture in Contemporary America* (Middletown, CT: Wesleyan University Press, 1994).

12.

When You Grow Up?

Adolescents and a Call to the Way of Life Abundantly

ALMEDA M. WRIGHT

Almeda M. Wright is Assistant Professor of Religion and Education at the Yale Divinity School. Her research focuses on African American religion, adolescent spiritual development, and the intersections of religion, education, and public life. Her publications include *The Spiritual Lives of Young African Americans* and *Children, Youth, and Spirituality in a Troubling World*.

What do you want to be when you grow up?

This remains one of the most prevalent questions related to adolescents and vocation. Even before the often paralyzing and panic-inducing college selection processes of late high school, most teens have suffered through school assignments where they were asked just this question. And the expected answers outline some list of acceptable professions they aspire to – lawyer, doctor, teacher, singer, artist, and in my case from sixth grade forward, electrical engineer.

Christian communities have our own variation on this question. We ask (or at least they did in my small, rural Virginia church), *What do you feel called to do? Where do you think God is calling you? What does God want for your/my/our life?* Often there is an equally expected set of responses.

Having expectations is not wrong, and our discussions of calling and vocation are important. In truth, much of what we do in children's and youth ministry goes beyond cultivating knowledge *of* faith in order to help children and youth *live* integrated, spirit-led lives.

However, whenever I am asked to discuss or think about vocation across the life cycle, I am struck by how often our conversations assume a certain quality of life and level of resources that so many populations – across the globe and in our own backyards – do not have, particularly the most vulnerable among us. Far too often, conversations about vocation and even ministry take for granted basic material and psychological resources. Too often, ministry goes forward as if we can assume that the only things children, youth, and their families need from faith leaders are spiritual nurture and help discerning what they want to be when they grow up. I have been challenged by the erroneous assumptions that we make about the kids we encounter each week in youth group, in Sunday schools, in our classrooms, in our community outreach, or even the ones cutting through the parking lot but who would never come into our church buildings. I also think about the ones we fail to see and who are not privileged to be a part of an established caring community such as a church or a team.

Children and youth have been reminding us that we cannot operate like this anymore. This chapter explores some of the narratives of young people we often don't hear from, and it begins to dream more about how our ministries can grow when we attend to the "voices of the least of these!" as well as the kids we do see (and who we might call the better off, if not the well off).

Challenges to "When I grow up..."

What's so wrong with asking kids what they want to be when they grow up? Not only was I asked this question when I was in my teen years, but as an adult I've also posed it to children and adolescents in my family and my church. We want young people to know that we care about them. We want them to be aware that we're invested in their lives and in their prospects for a future in which they flourish.

But although we might pose this question frequently, is it really the question we should be asking?

In addition to discovering how often we ask this question, I also found an array of responses that challenge both the nature of the question and the assumptions about the lived realities of children and youth that are embedded in the question. Here, I draw on examples from popular culture (in the form of cartoons), the narratives of a few young people, and practical theological texts.

First, there is the brilliantly witty *Peanuts* comic strip in which Charlie Brown and Linus are discussing what they want to be in the future. Linus says he wants to be "outrageously happy."[1] This in many ways is the perfect response – most would love a life in which outrageous happiness was the state of our future. In this classic cartoon, we have a critique of the idea that our future aspirations should primarily concern employment or work. There is a reminder that emotional well-being should accompany whatever we do. It should also be of primary concern when we imagine our futures and our life callings. Linus is pointing to one of many problems implicit with typical responses to the question of what one wants to be when one grows up.

One of another, more sinister, set of comic strips shows adults asking young people what they want to be when they grow up. The response? ALIVE![2] (The larger contexts for this set include discussions about "school shootings" and ongoing wars.) The cartoons were created by South African cartoonist Zapiro in 2006. He was responding to a series of schoolyard murders in that country. However, I observed this particular comic strip shared via social media after the shooting deaths of young people on the way to school in Chicago, after Sandy Hook, and after other shooting deaths of young people at the hands of police officers or vigilantes in the United States. The cartoon makes a scathing critique of the reality that children and adolescents cannot take for granted that they will grow up, or have a future.

These contrasting responses are not limited to popular culture or political cartoons. When I listen to narratives of young poets and teens around the United States, I encounter young African Americans who also write about death and violence more often than they write of personal triumphs and dreams for their futures. One young woman, Alexis Pettis, penned a poem which began with her singing:

Hush little baby, don't you cry
Your tears won't make you stay alive
If you scream no one will hear
You'll be gone in an early year[3]

As I listened to her perform this poem, I could sense the collective inhale of the people in the audience as they wrestled with how to respond to her words. Her poem continues with discussions about the probability of death for her or for teens like her *and* about the fact that, in many ways, death seems more inviting than facing myriad oppressions as a young Black woman in the United States.

Similarly, in a recent youth ministry text, Katherine Turpin and Anne Carter Walker share the narratives of adolescent boys who are asked about their dreams for their future. One young man, Casey, who comes from a more affluent community, responds with amazing zeal and remarks, "The question I have is: Is it better to try to save the whole world, or to work on one thing at a time?" Turpin and Walker contrast Casey's response to another young man, Andre, who comes from a non-dominant community. When asked, *What dreams do you have for yourself at 35?* Andre simply responds, "I hope I'm still alive when I'm 35."[4] Andre wasn't the only young person who responded that they simply hoped to be alive in the future.[5]

Turpin and Walker carefully outline the divergent ways each young man comes to conversations about vocation, based on their lives up to this point:

Andre's biggest question...reflected concern for the very existence of his life as a young, African-American male who saw few avenues for breaking the cycle of violence in the world around him. For Andre, issues of...vocation are about sheer survival. This isn't to say that Andre isn't, or shouldn't be, concerned about social transformation as a piece of vocation, but that such vocational concerns arise directly from his experiences of poverty, pain, and violence...Casey, by contrast, reflects a commonly-held, middle class, dominant culture approach to vocation. Casey's statement reflects a stable material environment, so that choosing to attempt to "save the world" becomes possible in his mind...he demonstrates confidence in his ability to use his own power to affect change in the world...[6]

Other scholars who reflect with youth note that those youth have no straight-forward or taken-for-granted assumptions about their futures and their lives. From a somewhat different perspective, pastoral theologian Gregory Ellison recounts the experiences of African-American adolescent men from across socio-economic statuses who embody what Ellison calls the state of being "cut dead but still alive." In this state, a person is rendered invisible and is seemingly unnoticed by the larger social forces.[7]

Similarly, religious educator Patrick Reyes offers a rich narrative exploration of his struggle and primary calling to live among Latino youth.[8] Again, the question of what one wants to be when one grows up takes on a very different tone when one is combatting social or psychic invisibility, disconnection, and hopelessness, and is battling just to live.

Changing Developmental Realities

The juxtaposition of these responses to seemingly innocuous questions about one's future reminds us that our assumptions regarding adulthood and maturation are not as informed with reality as we would hope for or would like. Neither are they as we had presumed them to be in generations past. Current political cartoons and youth narratives are forcing us to reconsider the question, *What do you want to be when you grow up?* within the contexts in which adolescents are coming of age. The cartoons and narratives are stark reminders that stable, middle class economic realities are non-existent for many young people, and that poverty, violence, death, and a culture of disposability are very real for other youth.[9]

Stage-based theories of adolescent development most often point to young people wrestling with questions of both identity and vocation: who they will be, and what they want to do. Erroneously, the hope was that a stable material reality would serve as the marker of adulthood (and the fulfillment of the American Dream). Therefore, youth workers needed simply to lead young people to contemplate meaningful full-time work and/or healthy, stable relationships as the response to these questions of identity.[10] However, we are now forced to rethink how young people are maturing and growing as theorists more fully attend to the psycho-social, cultural, and political dimensions of how young people understand themselves and their futures. For example, in a recent study of the *personal theologies* of young adults in the United States, William Gortner shifts the developmental conversation away from *Who am I?* in order to explore the other questions that many young adults are pondering, such as, *Where am I? What kind of world have I inherited?* and *What kind of world would I like to inhabit?*[11]

Changing Perspectives on Christian Vocations

In addition to asking what one would like to be when one grows up, the conversation within Christian communities and religious education persists in asking similar questions, including questions about our hopes, aspirations, identities, and responsibilities as followers of Christ. William Placher's work, *Callings,* attests to over 20 centuries of Christian discussions surrounding vocations, callings, and identity related to being disciples of the revolutionary messiah, Jesus. Placher notes that, from the beginning of the Christian movement, the response to questions of what God's calling was for humanity (or even individuals) directly connected with the social reality lived in at the time. For example, early Christians wrestling with callings to a Christian life had to figure out *if* they were going to be followers of Jesus *and* how they would make this declaration and commitment known publicly. Then, as now, responding to the call to Christian life required wrestling with how one would live in light of one's commitment to Christ. However, as more people became Christian, over time the emphasis of vocation shifted to wrestling with a call to "religious life," say as a monk or nun. And Placher notes other shifts that happened after the Reformation, such as rethinking every job and every part of our workaday life as part of the calling of Christ.[12]

Today, there is no easy categorization of how Christians primarily view calling and vocation. Therefore, we see notions of call that reflect each of these historical emphases, among others. But the historical perspectives on calling and vocation only partially prepare us to walk with young people, particularly those youth who do not feel that they have the luxury of wrestling with *what they will be* when the more pressing question is *if they will be*. Therefore, we have to reconsider the historical ways that Christian communities have discussed callings and vocation, in order to better attend to the challenges contemporary adolescents are encountering. In other words, we have to ask anew how the call to be Christian helps us to respond to the material and psychic realities of violence, poverty, and oppression – as well as to the overabundance of material goods in a smaller part of the population.

The reality is that youth worker training and youth formation in religious communities have often fallen short of attending to the diversity of lived experiences that young people are encountering. And despite our best efforts, religious communities have often re-inscribed the values and structures of dominant Western culture instead of walking with youth as they discern what God is saying to them. When we think of discussions of vocation with young people we must fully understand that, while there may be developmental and spiritual similarities across broad spectrums of young people, their individual contexts and life circumstances heavily influence what hopes they aspire to and what hurdles they must overcome in order to live.

The examples from popular culture and youth ministry research remind us that conversations regarding vocation go much deeper than simply walking with young people as they select a particular career path. Conversations regarding vocation and calling push us to look closely at the material, psychic, and spiritual realities of young people. They demand that we attend to the needs and gifts of youth as well as to the disparities in their material and psychic realities, which manifest in very different assumptions regarding what's possible in their lives and what they can even begin to hope for.

Although the responses and dreams of Andre and Casey seem to be at opposite ends of the spectrum of what we encounter with young people, in truth their responses are not that extreme. And divergence in narratives is increasing, even if youth workers are not prepared to address it. Far too often, when we become aware of the different challenges and lived realities of particular youth the task becomes that of getting them (and all young people) to our idea of the ideal place. We often wrestle with trying to figure out how to level the playing field so that all youth can have a fair, or at least better, opportunity for success in their lives and in their futures.

However, is it actually possible for us to allow for different pictures of success and well-being, for different measures of success? This is the more difficult challenge, and one that I don't fully have answers or responses to. This challenge requires walking with young people toward never-before-seen outcomes rather than pushing them toward our own pre-defined solutions. We have failed to attend to the contours of the lived realities of young people as we purport to do ministry with them. As a result, we have to find ways to nurture different dreams. But first we must cultivate practices that allow us to hear and see differences in ways that do not label different as deficient.

Called to Live! The Christian Witness of Choosing Life

Reflecting on the diverse responses to the questions of what young people want to be when they grow up and what types of dreams they have for themselves, I feel the despair of both youth who are overwhelmed by privilege and those who are overwhelmed with violence and poverty.

However, I also hear the wisdom of the African-American Christian tradition that pushes us to "hope against hope" and trust that there is a God who calls and *makes a way out of no way*. Ironically, the wisdom of this tradition is not always clearly echoed in the witness of elders or adults. Instead, as I recount in other writings, the wisdom of adolescents within and around communities of faith often offers the best reminder of the truth of these traditions. Yes, even as I research and write about the concerns of adolescents, I esteem adolescents as exemplars of faith and life for other teens and adults. In particular, I often return to the witness and narrative of Kira, another African-American adolescent who daily encountered death and violence such that most adults have not experienced.[13]

Kira is an amazing young woman who I dared to listen with and to, and who has contributed so much to my life. As a 16-year-old, she helped me reshape how I approach ministry with youth who experience violence and oppression. She stretched my understanding of theology and my practices of faith. For example, her confidence in who God is and how God could transform situations forced me to wrestle with larger understandings of God and, in particular, God's gift of abundant life through Jesus Christ. Kira reminded me that even in the face of violence, death, and death-dealing systems, the Christian witness through individuals and churches is still important. In particular, her approach to issues of violence and death was spiritual, but not in an escapist manner. She wanted young people around her to experience the love of God and others. She wanted them to desire life and to choose to live abundantly, instead of perpetuating the cycles of violence that seemed almost predetermined given the material and psychic realities of her community. In her responses to the questions of what she wanted to be when she grew up and what she was doing now in the face of the violence and despair around her, she affirmed that she felt called to witness, pray, and live in such a way that she "took the limits off" what God could do in her life, and in the lives of others through her.

It was a teenaged girl who reminded me that the call of Christ to all young people is that Jesus comes that they might have life and have it more abundantly. This call is not determined by their starting place in life, or limited by our ineffective efforts at ministry with youth in and from diverse realities. While there are myriad books about discernment with youth and walking with youth as they continue to listen for the calling(s) in their lives, the most powerful call, which lies at the core of reflecting on call and vocation with adolescents in a society that seems overwhelmed with despair and disparities, is the call to life and life more abundantly.

In many ways we hear echoes of this call in the Hebrew Bible (Deut 30:15-20) with the affirmation that, when a choice had been placed before the people of Israel – a choice between life and death, blessings and curses – they were admonished to choose life. Likewise, the call to abundant life gets introduced (in those particular terms) in the Gospel of John, with Jesus offering the dichotomy between what the thief comes to do and what Jesus offers (Jn 10:10).

The use of the word *choice* should in no way imply that simply believing differently or making a decision to live is going to change the reality. But it's a reminder that part of what it means for young people to address systems of oppression and discern ways to live includes addressing what they see as possible and what they feel empowered to do. More specifically, remembering the abundant life that God desires for their lives is necessary in order to counter a narrative that lets them imagine only death. It is part of reminding them that they have the power – not arrogance or unrealistic hubris – to push back against death-dealing systems, and that churches and Christian communities are going to work alongside them to protest systems and structures that do not afford them the opportunities to live into the promises God makes for their lives.

Called to Abundant Life!

Discerning vocation with youth from diverse backgrounds starts by inviting them (again) to Christ's call to the way of life abundantly. The concept of abundant life has a long and complicated history. Often I get into trouble when I begin talking about a call to abundant life, primarily because during the mid-20th century this idea became synonymous with teachings about spiritual growth, material prosperity, and physical healing.[14] Far from being a fully-articulated doctrine or theology, the call to abundant life draws on varied interpretations of words attributed to Jesus in John 10:10, where Jesus states that his purpose for coming to earth was so that all could have life abundantly: "The thief comes only to steal and kill and destroy. I came that they may have life, and have it abundantly."[15] Abundant life, or a way of life abundantly, is not simply a set of truths to espouse or a theology to believe in. It is our best approximation of what we are called to as Christian communities. Thomas Groome argues that in John 10, Jesus is echoing the same wisdom he offered to his disciples when he taught them to pray, saying, "Thy kingdom come on earth as it is in heaven."[16] In other words, Jesus is pointing toward an understanding of the ultimate vision of God.

However, these seemingly simple statements of what God intends for our lives are overwhelming in that they offer different visions of both what is possible for our lives and what things we must strive toward. (They may even be more overwhelming than the hopelessness and despair we hear from an Andre, and they may be possible only with the youthful zeal of a Casey.) At the same time, other articulations of abundant life remain insufficient as well, in that they reduce abundant life to spiritual concerns and fail to address lived realities. Therefore, I, with Kira, Andre, and even Casey, ask: *How do we foster, among all youth, a way of life abundantly that addresses the realities of violence, poverty, and dehumanization?*

Called to Live and Participate Now

Kira's reminder of the call to a way of life abundantly in the face of realities that challenge many youth, some of whom do not even know if they will grow up, also reminds us to reject the tendency (well-meaning or otherwise) to approach conversations with adolescents regarding vocation and call primarily from the perspective of what youth *will become*. Instead, we must address what youth *are called to right now*. The push for congregations to remove the lens, or in Kira's words, to take the limits off "future calling" reminds us of the developmental *and* spiritual readiness of adolescents to discern what God is asking of their lives and to contribute meaningfully to the work of God and to their communities *now*. For example, positive youth developmental theories recommend that young people have opportunities to contribute meaningfully as full partners to their families and communities. We see this manifest as the community service requirement in most schools in affluent communities. We also see it manifest in less affluent communities as the reality that most teens already work or help out in their families.

However, there is also a strong biblical witness regarding the ability of young people to contribute meaningfully to the life of faith as young people, and not "when they grow up".[17] Far too often, the expectation – or even ideal – is that young people should be pushed into the wings of their own lives and communities instead of being invited into productive ways to consider the calling that God issues to each of us from the time that we are born. Part of thinking about Christian understandings of calling and vocation with adolescents is moving out of their way so that they can begin to work and act in ways that more fully approximate those of the beloved community that we are called to as part of the body of Christ.

So what does walking with young adults at these extreme places look like? How can religious communities and youth workers attend to the range of dreams and realities? While careful prayer and tremendous work are required in order to eradicate disparities, some strategies for choosing life and living the way of life abundant with all youth include:

- *Listening to youth (to their differences and their lived realities) and teaching youth to listen to the world around them;*
- *Expanding our dreams and markers of success, so that middle class success isn't the primary image, and so that we don't forget that many youth do not have this as an immediate option;*
- *Offering young people a reminder that, even if their material and psychic realities offer them little in the way of hope for life, there is still a God who wants the best for them;*[18]
- *Creating communities of faith that support young people in their work to LIVE, and working to transform systems that keep other youth from living.*

Even as these strategies offer both simple and complex suggestions for action, the larger reminder is for congregations and youth workers to continue in the work of walking with all youth as they try to respond to the call of God to live. It requires us to pray with Howard Thurman his prayer asking for the courage to live:

> *Give me the courage to live!*
> *Really live – not merely exist.*
> *...gracious God, hear my prayer:*
> *Give me the courage to live!*[19]

This prayer reflects the deep yearning of all those youth who are discerning not just what they want to be in the future, but also what they can do and say about their lived realities now. Within the call to live and the prayer for the courage to live lies the understanding that life and living are not things that we should take for granted. Clearly, there are realities and circumstances, some of our own making and others inherited, that inhibit us or limit our opportunities. As a result, living is something that requires courage and boldness; it is difficult work.

Attending to the diversity of lived realities requires that we walk with adolescents as they choose and discern how to live now, that we pray with them Thurman's prayer to "give me the courage to live!" So instead of asking young people what they want to be when they grow up, we might ask them how they are called to live abundantly today. How are they going to respond to the call to live today?

Portions of this essay were previously published in Almeda M. Wright, *The Spiritual Lives of Young African Americans* (New York: Oxford University Press, 2017).

1. See Peanuts Cartoon Strip, *Reno Evening Gazette*, January 11, 1960. Quote Page 11 (NArch Page 3), Reno, Nevada. (NewspaperArchive).
2. Zapiro, "Five schoolyard murders in just eight months" http://www.zapiro.com/061011indep. (accessed September 12, 2017).
3. Alexis Pettis *Louder than a Bomb* Poem, https://www.youtube.com/watch?v=YBkScA0WL2c (published March 16, 2014).
4. Katherine Turpin and Anne Walker Carter, *Nurturing Different Dreams: Youth Ministry across Lines of Difference* (Eugene, OR: Pickwick, 2014), 35.

5. Ibid., 3.

6. Ibid., 35.

7. Gregory C. Ellison, *Cut Dead but Still Alive: Caring for African American Young Men* (Nashville: Abingdon, 2013), 1-6.

8. See Patrick Reyes, *Nobody Cries When We Die: God, Community, and Surviving to Adulthood* (St. Louis: Chalice, 2016).

9. See Henry A. Giroux, *Fugitive Cultures: Race, Violence, and Youth* (New York: Routledge, 1996) for a fuller discussion of a culture of disposability, and Henry A. Giroux, *Stealing Innocence: Corporate Culture's War on Children* (New York: Palgrave, 2000), 8.
   See also Almeda Wright, "The Kids are Alright: Rethinking Problem-based approaches to Adolescent Spirituality," *Journal of Youth and Theology* 14, no. 1 (2015): 91-110. Additionally, the question remains problematic in that the primary responses focus on an individual creating choices for their own life or future. The question makes no assumption or demands regarding how a young person will contribute to the world. Turpin and Walker, along with many other theorists, offer scathing critiques both of our understandings of adolescence and of our ministries with them as they are often geared toward "middle class values" that entertain youth, instead of inviting them to contribute.

10. See Erik H. Erikson's discussion of identity and the life cycle in *The Life Cycle Completed*, reissued edition (W. W. Norton & Company, 1994).
    See also Friedrich L. Schweitzer, *The Postmodern Life Cycle: Challenging for Church and Society* (St. Louis: Chalice, 2004).

11. See David T. Gortner, *Varieties of Personal Theology: Charting The Beliefs And Values Of American Young Adults* (Burlington, VT: Ashgate, 2013).
    Other developmental theorists and theologians note the sociological and communal emphasis on youth development and identity. My assertion here is not that this is a new way of looking at adolescent development; however, the models of healthy adolescence still reflect assumptions from the dominant culture with minimal reworking to account for the varied experiences of contemporary adolescents.
    Several theologians, such as Fowler, Thurman, and Buechner, who have influenced my understanding of vocation offer definitions which attend to the communal and sociological dimensions of calling.

12. William C. Placher, *Callings: Twenty Centuries of Christian Wisdom on Vocation* (Grand Rapids: Eerdmans, 2005).

13. Kira's narrative and parts of the discussion of the call to abundant life are more fully discussed in Almeda M. Wright, *The Spiritual Lives of Young African Americans* (New York: Oxford University Press, 2017).

14. These teachings became popular through the ministry and media of Oral Roberts. See David Edwin Harrell, Jr., *Oral Roberts: An American Life* (Bloomington: Indiana University Press, 1985) for a larger history of Oral Roberts' ministry. Also the current ministry and university website are full of references to abundant life and interconnected teachings on the belief in miracles and in material wealth and healings.

15. New Revised Standard Version.

16. Thomas H. Groome, *Will There Be Faith? A New Vision for Educating and Growing Disciples* (New York: HarperOne, 2011), 23.

17. See Almeda M. Wright, "Reflective Youth Ministry: Youth Ministry as Ongoing, Critical, Communal Reflection," in *Adoptive Youth Ministry: Foundations for Youth Ministry*, edited by Chap Clark (Grand Rapids: Baker Academic, 2016), 85-96.

18. According to Thomas Groome, abundant life, or the fullness of life, is what God intends for all. Groome writes "God intends the best of everything for everyone, all the time, and the integrity of God's creation" (Groome, *Will There Be Faith?* 23). See Groome, *Will There Be Faith?* for a fuller discussion.

19. Howard Thurman, "What Shall I Do With My Life?" in *A Strange Freedom*, ed. Walter Earl Fluker and Catherine Tumber (Boston: Beacon, 1998), 30-34.

13.

Bread on the Water

AMY K. BUTLER

Rev. Amy K. Butler is the Senior Minister at The Riverside Church in Manhattan. She holds several degrees, and has worked as director at a homeless shelter for women in New Orleans and served at St. Charles Avenue Baptist Church in New Orleans, and Calvary Baptist Church in Washington, DC.

At our 2015 Faith Forward gathering in Chicago, the Rev. Dr. Amy Butler closed our time together with a sermon. As you prepare to put this book down and go forward in your work with children, youth, and families, reflect deeply on the words that she shares.

If you were one of the 400 people who attended the inaugural Faith Forward event, you may recall that it was held at the church I was serving at the time, Calvary Baptist in Washington, DC. I've been part of the Faith Forward advisory team since the beginning. And over the years, it has been a joy to return to a place filled with light and life and optimism and hope; to hear about the amazing things that so many creative leaders are doing in their work; to think creatively about our future; to look forward, you might say.

Looking forward is really at the heart of our collective work at Faith Forward, isn't it? We follow a God who is ever-creating, and most of the time we're just doing the best we can to keep up.

And looking forward has certainly been a theme of my year. In fact, last year in Nashville at Faith Forward, I was just reaching the end of a pretty gruelling vocational discernment process with The Riverside Church in the City of New York. As I learned, Riverside has an incredible legacy of prophetic voice and cutting-edge ministry. It's an extra-denominational Christian experiment. Throughout its history, it has led the way for radical expressions of Christianity on many fronts. It's an "on the ground" expression of the kinds of big questions we're all asking.

I couldn't have had any idea at that time last year of how my life would change in this year gone by (and that's probably another chapter, or a three volume tell-all memoir, or something like that). What began for me in that process of discernment has continued throughout this year: *a relentless push to find answers to the question of where the church is going; a persistent offer to speak to the desperation that many in the institutional church are feeling right now; a willingness to take on leadership of what some might say is among the most formidable congregations in American Protestantism today.*

While I, along with everybody else, had been asking theoretical questions about the future of the church, real life intersected with those questions in a big way when, shortly after Faith Forward last year, Riverside voted to call me as their senior minister.

And so the ball started rolling. I said goodbye to a congregation I had loved for 11 years. I packed up and moved to New York City, while my two youngest children – then older teenagers – stayed in DC to finish up their final years of high school. I began the work of learning a new congregation, city, set of responsibilities...all the while looking forward, forward, forward to whatever was next, to the dream of the future, to all the possibilities God might create in this wonderful work.

I was doing all of this, speeding along, thrilled by the challenge of the work and the wild ride, and trying desperately to juggle all the changes in my family's life and learn all the things I had to learn. And then a few weeks ago I found myself, as part of this journey, travelling to Spokane, Washington to deliver a lecture.

It was spring break for my youngest kids, Hannah and Sam, so I thought it would be fun to take them with me. I was hoping we could have some family time on the West coast. So we packed up and headed toward the Pacific. I explained to the kids all the obligations I would have that week and when I thought we might fit in some leisure time, and I worked the whole flight out to Washington. I was so busy and preoccupied that the first day on the ground my phone somehow slipped out of my hand and fell face down onto the cement sidewalk. It completely shattered on impact.

I don't know if you would feel the same dread that I felt when that happened, but there it was: in one fateful second my connection to all that was "important" was ripped from me.

As it turns out, Spokane is a bit of a small town. They have an Apple store, thanks be to God, but for some reason still unknown to me, the fine folks at the store couldn't replace my phone right away. They had to order it. And it would take three days for a new one to arrive.

THREE DAYS??!! This is the United States of America, people!

So I struggled through. The kids came along to my speaking gig, simultaneously baffled that anyone would voluntarily show up to hear me say anything and desperately bored out of their minds. Hannah, my almost-18-year-old, graciously offered me the use of her phone so my colleagues could reach me, and I was using it the very next morning when we were at Riverside State Park. We were walking along the Spokane River in one of the most beautiful natural settings I'd been in in a long time when I opened the camera app on the phone and took a picture of my kids, who were walking ahead of me. It was in that moment that I suddenly came to myself.

Okay, maybe it wasn't that biblical.

But I looked at that scene and had one thought: *Right here is what matters the most right now*. Those two young lives are, in this moment, right here in my very presence. Those two lives about to launch into independence and a new kind of relationship with me – adult to adult –

are here with each other and with me in this beautiful, amazing place. I need to be here, right here, with them, now.

I put the phone away.

In the weeks that followed this experience, I returned again and again to the book of Ecclesiastes, that part of our holy text that nobody ever hears or reads unless they're die hard Pete Seeger fans. Ecclesiastes is a bit difficult to get our minds around. It's not that fun for biblical historical scholars either because nobody really knows who wrote it, when it was written, or why. Further, it's full of deep-sounding statements that reflect a depth of wisdom we don't often live as we skate through our lives on the surface.

In chapter 11, the writer of Ecclesiastes muses about the value of exactly what I felt in that moment, something I'd venture to say we all grapple with, especially those of us who are persistently struggling to birth a future we cannot fully see. The sage of Ecclesiastes seems to be speaking directly to me – to us – when he says, "As you do not know the path of the wind, or how the body is formed in a mother's womb, so you cannot understand the work of God, the maker of all things. Sow your seed in the morning, and at the evening let your hands not be idle, for you do not know which will succeed, whether this or that, or whether both will do equally well" (Ecc 11:5-6).

Here.

Be right here. In this moment, for this very time.

Look deeply into the eyes of the person right in front of you. Feel the brush of another's hand on yours. Savour the hug of a friend. Listen with your whole self. Be open to be changed by what you receive.

Be. Here. Now.

Those of us who work with youth, children, and families, and those of us who work within an institution with an unknown future are constantly being challenged to look ahead. And it's true: we are important actors who are shaping a future for the church when we create the kinds of environments that are imagined in the collision of ideas and practices at Faith Forward, and offered throughout this book. These are environments where young disciples can wonder about the

Divine, and where we can offer opportunities whereby they are shaped into people of faith who live lives of justice, generosity, and action.

Our children and youth are becoming – as we all are as long as there is breath in our bodies. But those precious lives intersect our own right here, right now. And I think it may be right, as we prepare to return to our communities of service, energized for what's ahead, if we pause to savour the moments with them that are right in front of us. I think it may be right to delight in the discoveries of our littlest ones, to honour their wisdom and leadership, and to cherish this moment – this one right now – before it's gone.

Some versions of the Ecclesiastes text I shared earlier start with a translation of verse one that reads: "Ship your grain upon the sea..." And there are others that read: "Send out your bread upon the waters..." As I read the text, thinking about these moments that matter, I reflected again on the time that has passed since we were last together.

Last year on my way home from Faith Forward I was in line at the taxi cab stand at National airport when my mother called my cell phone. I couldn't understand her very well with the noise of the traffic around me, but I heard enough to know that my younger brother, 38 years old, was in the hospital. They didn't know what was wrong, but it seemed bad. "Stay tuned," I heard.

The next few weeks were a blur as I, along with my other siblings, flew to Hawaii to be with my parents and my brother and his family. Later that week, we had to make the hard decision to remove my brother John from life support and say goodbye far, far too soon.

The months that followed my brother's death, as I mentioned earlier, were filled with my personal transition to a new city and new job. The background narrative that not many people knew was that my sister-in-law was struggling to parent four young children alone, and my other siblings were stepping up to help her care for them. I, of course, couldn't help in the ways that they were helping. I couldn't change diapers and drive carpool and pack lunches. I was barely surviving my own transition. And all of us were trying to navigate the waves of grief that kept dunking us under at the most unexpected moments.

Late last fall, my sister-in-law visited New York City with my littlest nephew, Grady. He looks so much like my brother John that every time I looked at him my breath would catch and my throat would close and tears would threaten. I wanted to fix things for him, for them, for all of us, so very much.

One fall afternoon I took Grady to Central Park for a walk and to feed the ducks. We packed the stroller with a picnic blanket and some stale bread and walked down to the lake in the middle of the park. I didn't know it then, but the ducks in Central Park are not very hungry. At least they weren't last fall. We'd throw the bread out into the lake and they'd totally ignore it. They seemed to treat it as a passing nuisance rather than a free meal. The bread would land on the surface of the water and just sink to the bottom. I was furious.

Furious.

I had this one afternoon with my nephew, during which I'd wanted so much to show him how to feed the ducks. I'd wanted to soak in every little bit of my precious brother in this little person, to patch up the gaping hole of loss my nephew didn't even know he was carrying, to make everything better. But the ducks didn't care and wouldn't cooperate. And I felt defeated.

Until I felt a little hand on my cheek. My nephew snuggled up on my lap and pointed out an airplane in the sky, trying out new words and taking in fascinating wonders all around him. He was secure in my arms in that moment and just fine. He didn't care about the ducks. He couldn't know the weight of the world around him. He just knew in that moment that he was safe and loved, and that from that place of security there were more discoveries than he could imagine all around him.

The ducks didn't cooperate. And I can't fix Grady's future, a life without his dad by his side. But I could be there, right there, in that moment. And I could feel his hand on my cheek. And I could witness his amazement. And I could feel hope and possibility through my tears.

I'm pretty sure the writer of Ecclesiastes was not talking about feeding recalcitrant ducks in Central Park when he wrote, "send out your bread upon the waters." But it became a metaphor for something he was surely trying to convey: *This life is so precious. The moments we have with our children are moments of deep meaning, not just for the future we're building, but for right now.* Right this very minute.

In all our hope for what will be, in all our striving to make it so, we should never neglect precious, breath-taking moments of becoming that are happening all around us and, indeed, within each one of us.

As you go from this place ready to move forward, ready to take all you have heard and learned and seen and put it into practice and change the world, I want to invite you (when you get home and before you commence changing the world) to send out some bread on the waters.

Sit in the reality of what is now. Witness the young lives around you in all the wonder that they are in this moment. See your own life through the lens of God's creative genius.

And give thanks.

For what a gift we have been given, these lives of ours.

Be here now.

Feel everything you can feel.

Witness the beauty all around you.

Send out your bread upon the water.

See God.

Amen.

ACKNOWLEDGEMENTS

It's hard to believe that Faith Forward has become what it is. Nearly a decade ago, when I thought about hosting some sort of conference for people seeking to engage in creative, forward-leaning ministry with young people, I never imagined that we would now be on the other side of our fifth gathering and third book. This volume, a compilation of presentations from the three most recent Faith Forward gatherings, only exists because of the tireless efforts and ardent support of so many.

Several people have served on the diverse leadership team of Faith Forward for one or more of the past three gatherings. Michael Novelli, to whom this book is dedicated, has been our event director for all of these events. He has supported our mission and kept us on track while also infusing these gatherings with compassion, creativity, and hope. Danielle Shroyer, Ivy Beckwith, Melvin Bray, Mark Novelli, Amy Butler, Daniel White Hodge, Michele Novelli, and Melanie Gordon have all offered their time and talents to our programming and advisory teams for many years, with support from Lilly Lewin, Rebekah Lowe, Romal Tune, and Kevin Alton. Thank you for sharing, honing, and spreading a vision of Faith Forward that's more beautiful than I could have imagined.

Several people have played crucial roles at various stages in this book's production. In particular, I'm grateful for the support of Pine Hill Divinity Hall at Atlantic School of Theology, who granted me two Leni Groeneveld Grants for Research Assistance. My research assistants, Kate Jones and Sr. Gemma MacLeod, provided invaluable help in transcribing presentations and proofreading chapters.

As always, Wood Lake Publishing has been a delight to work with on this book. Patty Berube, Debbie Joyal MacDonald, Mike Schwartzentruber, and Ellen Turnbull – among so many others on the team – have believed in the work of Faith Forward for many years. Thank you for continuing to support the collision of our missions.

These pages contain tremendous insight. The authors who generously share their lament, wisdom, and hope in this book are true gifts to the church. They look over the horizons and call us toward something new while continuing to honour and bring forward the best of our faith traditions. Thank you for painting these pages with words of challenge, encouragement, and inspiration.

THE CONTRIBUTORS

 Ivy Beckwith is Faith Formation Team Leader for the United Church of Christ. She is a speaker, consultant, and author. Her books include *Children's Ministry in the Way of Jesus* (with David Csinos), and *Postmodern Children's Ministry*. She holds degrees in English and Religious Education, and has held educational positions in churches throughout the United States.

 Marcia J. Bunge, Ph.D., is Professor of Religion and the Bernhardson Distinguished Chair of Lutheran Studies at Gustavus Adolphus College in Saint Peter, Minnesota. She has edited and contributed to four volumes on religious views of children, including *The Child in the Bible* and *The Child in Christian Thought*.

 Rev. Amy K. Butler is the Senior Minister at The Riverside Church in Manhattan. She holds several degrees, and has worked as director at a homeless shelter for women in New Orleans and served at St. Charles Avenue Baptist Church in New Orleans, and Calvary Baptist Church in Washington, DC.

 David M. Csinos is founder and president of Faith Forward. He currently serves as Assistant Professor of Practical Theology at Atlantic School of Theology in Halifax, Nova Scotia, Canada. Dave holds a PhD from University of St. Michael's College. He writes widely about faith formation, children's and youth ministry, and culture, and he is a popular speaker across the globe.

Daniel White Hodge, PhD, is a recognized urban youth culture expert and cultural literacy scholar. He is Associate Professor of Intercultural Communications and department chair of Communication Arts at North Park University in Chicago. His research interests are the intersections of faith, hip hop culture, race/ethnicity, and young adult emerging generations. www.whitehodge.com.

Brian D. McLaren is an author, speaker, activist, public theologian, and passionate advocate for "a new kind of Christianity." He is an Auburn Senior Fellow, a contributor to We Stand With Love, and a leader in the Convergence Network. His books include *The Great Spiritual Migration* and *We Make the Road by Walking*.

Waltrina N. Middleton is a preacher, poet, social critic, and community organizer committed to actualizing the vision of a Beloved community. She serves as the Associate Dean of the Andrew Rankin Memorial Chapel, and is actively engaged in social justice issues domestically and throughout the diaspora. She is founder and organizer of Cleveland Action.

Rev. Dr. Otis Moss III is Senior Pastor of Trinity United Church of Christ in Chicago and author of *Redemption in a Red Light District*, *The Gospel Re-Mix*, and *Blue Note Preaching in a Post-Soul World*. A highly regarded preacher, Rev. Dr. Moss is an ordained minister in the Progressive National Baptist Convention and the United Church of Christ.

Leslie Neugent is an ordained minister in the United Church of Christ and serves at Wayzata Community Church in Minnesota. In 2012, she launched a radically inclusive worship service and ministry called Parables. Leslie is author of *Red Fish Theology: A How-To Guide for Offering a Radically Inclusive Worship Service with the Special Needs Community.*

Eboo Patel is a leading voice in the movement for interfaith cooperation, and the Founder and President of Interfaith Youth Core. He holds a doctorate from Oxford University and served on President Obama's Inaugural Faith Council. He is a regular contributor to the public conversation around religion and religious pluralism in America.

Rev. Dr. Soong-Chan Rah is Milton B. Engebretson Professor of Church Growth and Evangelism at North Park Theological Seminary in Chicago, IL. He holds several degrees and is the author of numerous books, including *The Next Evangelicalism*, *Many Colors*, and *Prophetic Lament.*

Lisa Scandrette has devoted herself to a life of care, hospitality, and teaching children. She regularly facilitates workshops and provides administrative support for ReIMAGINE. In her spare time she loves creating with her hands.

Mark Scandrette is the founding director of ReIMAGINE: A Center for Integral Christian Practice. His books include *FREE* and *Soul Graffiti*. He frequently speaks, nationally and internationally, on creative, radical, and embodied Christian practice.

Almeda M. Wright is Assistant Professor of Religion and Education at the Yale Divinity School. Her research focuses on African American religion, adolescent spiritual development, and the intersections of religion, education, and public life. Her publications include *The Spiritual Lives of Young African Americans* and *Children, Youth, and Spirituality in a Troubling World.*

ALSO AVAILABLE FROM WOOD LAKE

Faith Forward

Volume 1

A DIALOGUE ON CHILDREN, YOUTH, AND A NEW KIND OF CHRISTIANITY

David M. Csinos and Melvin Bray, Editors

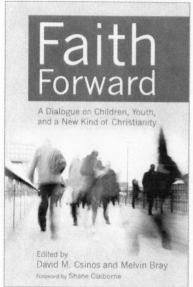

Knowing how to nurture faith in young people is a challenge, particularly when we want to encourage a faith that is generous, innovative, and contextual. Faith Forward gathers 21 presentations from the 2012 "Children, Youth, and a New Kind of Christianity" conference held in Washington, D.C., and makes them available for those in ministry with children and youth, pastors, parents, professors – anyone called to help young people on their journey of faith. Authors and attendees alike came from several countries and many denominational inflections. Likewise, the chapters express various contemporary takes on Christian faith and discipleship.

This book is a gold mine of information and inspiration for those seeking to engage children and youth in respectful conversation, exploration, and learning in today's complex world. If you are seeking grassroots, forward thinking, ecumenical, innovative, and collaborative ways to do children and youth ministry, then this book provides the material to move you in that direction.

Some contributing authors: Shane Claiborne, Brian McLaren, John H. Westerhoff III, Tony Campolo, Ivy Beckwith, Samir Selmanović, Joy Caroll Wallis.

288 PP | 6" X 9" PAPER | ISBN 978-1-77064-574-5
$29.95

ALSO AVAILABLE FROM WOOD LAKE

Faith Forward

Volume 2
RE-IMAGINING CHILDREN'S AND YOUTH MINISTRY

David M. Csinos and Melvin Bray, Editors

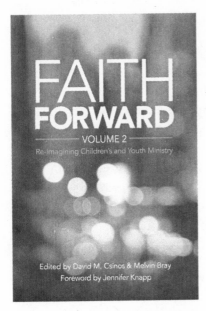

Faith Forward Volume 2: Re-Imagining Children's and Youth Ministry is the second volume in the groundbreaking "Faith Forward" series. Compiled from presentations given at the Faith Forward 2014 conference, held in Nashville, Tennessee, this volume features the work of Brian McLaren, Sandy Sasso, Andrew Root, Phyllis Tickle, Anne Wimberly, Ivy Beckwith, David M. Csinos, Paul-André Durocher, Bonnie Miller-McLemore, Melvin Bray, and more.

If you are seeking ways of doing children's and youth ministry that are grassroots, forward thinking, ecumenical, innovative and collaborative, this book will provide inspiration and wisdom for the journey. It is essential reading for leaders working with children and youth, as well as for pastors, professors, and parents – anyone and everyone seeking to engage children and youth in respectful conversation, exploration, and learning in today's complex world.

192 PP | 6" X 9" PAPER | ISBN: 978-1-77064-799-2
$19.95

WOOD LAKE

Imagining, living, and telling the faith story.

WOOD LAKE IS THE FAITH STORY COMPANY.

It has told
- the story of the seasons of the earth, the people of God, and the place and purpose of faith in the world;
- the story of the faith journey, from birth to death;
- the story of Jesus and the churches that carry his message.

Wood Lake has been telling stories for more than 35 years. During that time, it has given form and substance to the words, songs, pictures, and ideas of hundreds of storytellers.

Those stories have taken a multitude of forms – parables, poems, drawings, prayers, epiphanies, songs, books, paintings, hymns, curricula – all driven by a common mission of serving those on the faith journey.

Wood Lake Publishing Inc.
485 Beaver Lake Road
Kelowna, BC, Canada V4V 1S5
250.766.2778

www.woodlake.com